with love and blessings,
Sarah Ban Breathnach

MOVING ON:
CREATING YOUR
HOUSE OF BELONGING
WITH SIMPLE ABUNDANCE

MOVING ON:
CREATING YOUR HOUSE OF BELONGING WITH SIMPLE ABUNDANCE

BY SARAH BAN BREATHNACH

Meredith Books®
Des Moines, Iowa

Meredith Books
1716 Locust Street
Des Moines, Iowa 50309–3023
www.meredithbooks.com

Cover illustration: Mark Martullo

Back cover photograph: Brigitte Lacombe

Tree illustration: Margaret Chodos-Irvine

First Edition. Printed in the United States of America.
Library of Congress Control Number: 2005932222 ISBN: 0-696-22557-3

For My Husband

Jonathan Donahue Carr
With dearest love and deepest gratitude

Reams of Paper.
More than words can say.

CONTENTS

UPON READING THIS BOOK

If a reader cannot create a book along with the writer, the book will never come to life.

—Madeline L'Engle

As a passionate reader, I'm hard on books and other writers. Since I spend most of my waking hours in the company of words, I need books (my own included) to knock my socks off. Ravish my *résistance* with the first paragraph, or seduce me slowly through the introduction; as long as the feeling is intimate and immediate, I'm yours. I long to be bowled over by an author's insight, to wonder how I lived before her book explained it all to me or how the author knew me so well.

In reality, the books we love, the ones that really change the reader's life, are those that change the author's life as well. Chances are your favorite wordsmith hasn't got a clue what she'll write about when she begins. That's why she shows up for work every day; she is literally trying to figure out her life on the page. She thinks she's writing about eliminating clutter, but the Book knows better, and its hidden agenda will only be revealed in the fullness of time as the writer and reader work together. As far as I see it, my job is to get the words down on the page so that they can create a mystical bridge over the troubled waters of the unexpressed for both of us. Let the pages accumulate and they become a pilgrimage back to your future, and mine. As Milan Kundera so candidly confessed, "To be a writer does not mean to preach a truth, it means to discover a truth."

May I come in? Come in to your mind, heart, and home for a little while?

If you're perusing these pages, you're a kindred spirit who suspects, or at least hopes, that our shared passion—the pursuit of domestic bliss—is a truth much deeper than discovering the perfect paint chip or fabric swatch. (Although finding both has been known to make me gasp with delight!) I believe with all my heart that the pursuit of domestic bliss is a spiritual path, a sacred endeavor, and really, the road less traveled. I sense that you do too.

However, I've got to be honest with you before we begin. The truth that a woman's home is the most accurate barometer of her emotional, physical, psychological, and spiritual well-being can be as unsettling at times as it is reassuring. Nonetheless, the home is the surest diagnostic laboratory I've seen for discovering the deepest longings of the feminine soul and understanding how much time, creative energy, emotion, and nurturing She needs to be restored.

"You will express yourself in your house whether you want to or not," the mother of modern style, Elsie de Wolfe, declared in 1913. And what you will express is how well you take care of yourself. Not other people. I know you take care of everybody else in the world just fine. It's you I'm genuinely concerned about on these pages, as much as myself. You deserve to live in a home that embraces, nurtures, delights, and inspires you.

Part meditation, how-to-manual, and memoir, *Moving On* is for anyone who has ever wanted to reinvent her life and the space where she lives it. That's me, and perhaps you, too. It's about re-imagining the concept of home and our place in it. But it's also about how we cleverly, stubbornly, and subversively resist change until chaos or crisis engulfs us. How we thwart our deep desire for contentment day in and day out with domestic dishabille. I want to share with you the everyday epiphanies I've had through creating my own House of Belonging and the realization that it doesn't matter whom you live with or where you move from or to, you always take yourself with you. If you don't know who you are, or if you've forgotten or misplaced her, then you'll always feel as if you don't belong. Anywhere.

There's a fair chance that by the time a woman is 40, she will have moved house at least seven times in her life. Some of those moves will be considered "happy" ones, such as when she gets married; others will be moves forced upon her by catastrophic change, such as divorce. All moves are traumatic. Still, as writer Merle Shain observed, probably after unpacking in a new house, "It's hard to tell our bad luck from our good luck sometimes. Hard to tell sometimes for many years to come. And most of us have wept copious tears over someone or something when if we'd understood the situation better, we might have celebrated our good fortune instead."

There's a reason that moving ranks as the number one stressful rite of passage ahead of death, divorce, or debt. Maybe it's because moving is all of them simultaneously. Like Dante's *Inferno,* you descend from one circle of misery to another in slow, repetitive motion, only to drown in memory's quicksand. There have been many literary descriptions of hell through the ages, but most of them agree that the purpose of damnation is to punish those whose earthly behavior warrants it.

These days fire and brimstone don't scare me. But the mere sight of my new husband glancing at the real estate ads triggers tremors and trepidation. Last year I found myself moving four times and on both sides of the Atlantic. Despite the fact that my moves would have been considered by outsiders to be positive ones, quite frankly I was so disoriented, discombobulated, and discouraged that I feared not only for my soul but for my sanity.

While each move forced my head to wrestle with the myriad practical demands of uprooting one's life, my heart was forced to deal with five decades of denial. Not just of what went wrong in my life, but denial of how much had been right that I was unable to see because of clutter, mess, and disorder—the clutter of living surrounded by other people's choices for me; messes created through the best of intentions; and the cataclysmic disorder of the undone and the unsaid for the sake of appearances.

"Penetrate deeply into the secret existence of anyone about you, even of the man or woman whom you count happiest, and you will come upon things they spend all their efforts to hide," the Victorian novelist Myrtle Reed confessed just before she died in 1911. "Fair as the exterior may be, if you go in, you will find bare places, heaps of rubbish that can never be taken away, cold hearths, desolate altars and windows veiled with cobwebs."

Don't forget the brown cardboard boxes. You know, all those unmarked, unidentifiable parcels from the past that you can't bring yourself to part with. Where do you hide yours? In your attic, basement, utility room, garage, or that convenient catch-all underneath the stairs? What's in yours? Old clothes, photographs, diaries, and bric-a-brac? That's what I thought I'd find when moving became the catalyst that forced me to sort and sift through decades of rubble awaiting the reckoning.

Instead, I discovered scraps of shame, shreds of regret, and shards of self-reproach. Sins of omission and acts of self-sabotage. Physical evidence of errors, lapses of judgment, and cringe-worthy mistakes. Emotional flotsam and jetsam from different periods of my life, which had never been acknowledged, nor worked through, floated to the surface like personal belongings lost in a shipwreck. My unrecognized and unreconciled past was devastating in its demand to be dealt with at once, with dignity and compassion: years of rejection, overnight success, sudden wealth, harrowing debt, debilitating illness, marital indifference, great acclaim, unexpected divorce, an empty nest, private isolation, public scrutiny, and a lifetime of slovenly housekeeping. Some of those boxes I'd been moving from one place to another since I'd left for college; I hadn't known what to do with the stuff at 18, and I still didn't. Eventually I was forced to toss it. But only because the cost of shipping my adolescent artifacts as well as my grown daughter's childhood mementoes to England was prohibitive. Moving gives new meaning to the thought of one's past catching up with you.

Moving On is a book many of you have asked me to write for years—a creative and practical application of the Simple Abundance principles: gratitude, simplicity, order, harmony, beauty, and joy. But with a caveat: As we slowly move through the rooms of your home, we'll soothe your heart before redecorating, renovating, or restoring the place where you live. First the grace, then the fabric swatches.

During the writing of this book I realized that I no longer wanted to "paper over" the personal and emotionally charged issues each room revived, memories that I'd hidden from myself so skillfully. I wanted to honor them, hear their stories, let the room hear my version, let go, and then move on! The Simple Abundance principles became my go-betweens and helped me discover a profound serenity at home and a renewed sense of my authentic self, and I know they can bless you in the same way. Here's how.

Gratitude gives us the grace to face the emotional, psychological, and spiritual issues hidden in junk drawers and crowded closets.

Simplicity helps us streamline possessions and create a plan for homemaking that restores a satisfying and nurturing sense of rhythm to our daily round.

Order reveals how to create a space for everything we hold dear and how to distinguish between our needs and our wants.

Harmony teaches us how to decorate for comfort and use our senses to restore solace.

Beauty bestows visual delights throughout the house that bring us personal satisfaction.

Joy ensures that we come home not just to a dwelling place but to a shelter for our soul—a house where we belong.

The wonderful writer Katherine Paterson has observed that part of the magic of books is that "they allow us to enter imaginatively into someone else's life. And when we do that, we learn to sympathize with other people. But the real surprise is that we also learn truths about ourselves, about our own lives, that somehow we hadn't been able to see before." When those truths resonate for us, we say they "hit us where we live." That's why we're going to have to dig a little deeper than just between the lines, maybe meander through an emotional junk drawer or two, to see if we can't find what's missing in plain sight. If you're familiar with my other books, you'll know that personal archaeology is a recurring theme in my writing. There's a reason. It works. I'll be guiding you to the building site of your soul shelter with creative brainstorming suggestions on paper called "Do Try This At Home." We'll also be "playing house" with "Nesting Instincts."

Finally, at the end of each chapter you'll find a personal prayer that I've written especially for you inspired by my own soul searching for the House of Belonging. When you read them, or say them aloud, please remember, dearest friend, you are the Beloved I'm praying for. I hope you'll think of these end-of-chapter features as personal prompts to help you make sacred connections between the rooms of your house and all that still remains unresolved in your life. Imagine these pleasant diversions as psychic breathing spaces between the chapters; ponder and play with them.

I recommend that you read *Moving On* once through, and then go back and take your time reading each chapter while working on a particular area of your home. Like you, I'd love to have the guest bedroom be inviting for friends again, instead of an out-of-season clothing dump, but unless you really have company coming tomorrow, just keep the door closed. We'll get there, I promise.

However, I'm hoping that I can persuade you to linger

over these pages for a year, because I know for sure, you don't linger anywhere else. The simply abundant changes you will set in motion with this book are profound, and you need time to make them your own.

And while I can't guarantee that by the time we're finished you'll be cooking in Barbie's dream kitchen, my prayer for this book and your response to it is that maybe for the first time in your life, you won't want to trade places with any other woman because your own home will be so beautiful, comfortable, tidy, and serene. You'll realize no matter where you might reside at the moment, the home you have is all you need to shelter your dreams. Now. Not tomorrow or next year. That's because this is a book about discovering the crucial difference between letting go and moving on—in life, love, and houses.

So turn the page. Your homecoming starts here.

With all my love,
Sarah Ban Breathnach
Newton's Chapel
January 2006

This is the bright home
in which I live,
this is where
I ask
my friends
to come,
this is where I want
to love all the things
it has taken me so long
to learn to love...

There is no house
like the house of belonging.

—David Whyte

CHAPTER ONE

THE HOUSE OF BELONGING

ON WOMEN AND THEIR DREAM HOUSES

Between the Home set up in Eden, and the Home before us in Eternity, stand the Homes of Earth in long succession.

—Julia McNair Wright
(*The Complete Home*, 1879)

*T*he story of my heart begins with a tiny English cottage, paid for with the royalties from a book nobody in America wanted to publish.

Like many hopeful romantics, I have spent half a lifetime in a restless and relentless search for an elusive presence.

Anaïs Nin believed that "we travel, some of us forever, to seek other lives, other souls." Most of this time we think that the "other" we so desperately seek is our soul mate—the person we'd instantly recognize and feel completely comfortable with if our paths crossed. The one who'd finally give us the chance to smile, sigh, and say, *"I feel so at home with you!"*

For decades I thought that I could not become complete without such a union. I was right. But sacred partnerships arrive in our lives in many forms. Sometimes they're of wood and stone instead of flesh and bone. "I am as susceptible to houses as some people are susceptible to other human beings. Twice in my life I have fallen in love with one," the early 20th-century English writer Katharine Butler Hathaway confessed. "Each time it was as violent and fatal as falling in love with a human being."

The House of Belonging is an ancient Celtic metaphor for the body as the earthly home for our souls, as well as for the deep peace and feeling of safety, joy, and contentment found in intimate connections with people, places, and houses. My dear friend, John O'Donohue, the Irish poet and scholar, exquisitely explores these beautiful themes in his book *Anam Cara: A Book of Celtic Wisdom:* "When you learn to love and let yourself be loved, you come home to the hearth of your own spirit. You are warm and sheltered. You are completely at one in the house of your own longing and belonging."

I truly believe that we each have a House of Belonging waiting for us. Waiting to be found, waiting to be built, waiting to be renovated, waiting to be cleaned up. Waiting to rescue *us*. Waiting for the real thing: a grown-up, romantic, reciprocal relationship.

Every relationship you have—with other people, with your work, with Divinity—reflects in some way your soul's intimate union with you. Nowhere is this spiritual truth more apparent than in the relationships we have with our homes. All we have to do is take a good look around. Is your house tidy on the surface but hiding chaos and confusion in the cabinets and closets, or have you completely thrown down the towel onto a heap on the floor? "There are some homes you run from, and homes you run to," Laura Shaine Cunningham reminds us in her touching memoir, *Sleeping Arrangements*. In which direction are you running today?

The emotional attachment—good or bad—that we have to our home is a daily spiritual tutorial in Love. "Everyone longs for intimacy and dreams of a nest of belonging in which one is embraced, seen, and loved," John O'Donohue tells us. "Something within each of us cries out for belonging. We can have all the world has to offer in terms of status, achievement, and possessions, yet without a sense of belonging, it all seems empty and pointless."

When I glance back at my Gratitude Journal, I am astounded at how frequently "my beautiful home" has appeared there, no matter where I was living. It doesn't matter where *you* live today. You may be rooming in a motel or seeking sanctuary in a safe house halfway between your past and your future. You may even be without a roof to call your own, camping out on a friend's couch or community cot,

3

held hostage in a palace, or pitching a tent on the dark side of the moon. Heaven knows I've lived in some of those settings at one time or another. But the House of Belonging is your birthright; it is part of your Happily Ever After, whether you are married, single, divorced, widowed, with or without children. The blueprints of your House of Belonging exist as spiritual energy and hover over your head—ready, when you are, to be pulled down from Heaven to shelter your Soul on Earth. Each day, as Emily Dickinson says, you "dwell in possibility." You must believe this is true.

WITHOUT LOVE, WHERE WOULD YOU BE NOW?

The home is the centre and circumference, the start and the finish, of most of our lives.
—Charlotte Perkins Gilman

Why *do* we fall in love? Imagine someone whose face *lights* up every time he sees you coming toward him. How do you feel? Now imagine a house that does the same. From that first glance, the cottage, which was known as "Newton's Chapel," seemed so alive, warm, loving, and happy *to see me.* As if it had been waiting for *me.*

Still, whether it's human or house love, when our hearts first start racing, we rarely know whether this will be a lifelong union or a mad passionate interlude. The rites of courtship for both affairs of the heart seem so similar, a roller coaster of emotion: desire, approach, flirtation, wooing, infatuation, lust, bliss. One morning there's a knock at the front door; reality arrives telling us to "settle down now, settle down." If we can't, then rapture reluctantly gives way to acceptance or adjustment, change or estrangement, reconciliation or relinquishment. We move or move on.

"In literature and art, love is a myth we tell ourselves. By myth I mean not an invention or falsehood but rather a narrative that enfolds our deepest beliefs and longings. Love is the story we place above all others, the one we invest with the most value," Rosemary Sullivan ruminates in her brilliant exploration of women, passion, and romantic obsession, *Labyrinth of Desire* (which I think should be required reading for every woman). "I have come to believe that falling obsessively in love is one of life's necessary assignments. It cracks us open. We put everything at risk. In the process we discover the dimensions of our own appetites and desires. And life, to be lived fully, demands desire," Rosemary tells us. "Falling in love in this way will usually occur at a time of transition. We may not be conscious of it, but something has ended and something new must begin. Romantic obsession is a cataclysm breaking up the empty landscape." Perhaps when we fall in love at a glance, the question we really should be asking ourselves is *what is it that I'm longing for?* Or what is so lacking in my life that I need something different to shift the direction in which I'm going?

Rosemary Sullivan is meditating on the emotion women feel when they fall in love at first sight with men; I'm the one making the leap to house fever because I've succumbed to both. Suddenly, without warning (or so it seems) the trajectory of a woman's life changes, becoming "a vicarious route to some essential part of herself that she does not yet fully recognize or understand." The Beloved becomes "the heroic territory she longs to occupy."

She thinks she's found him—or home. Interestingly, the name of the greatest lover of all time, *Casanova*, means "new house."

MYSTICAL CHAIN OF CHANCE

How can you say luck and chance are the same thing? Chance is the first step you take, luck is what comes afterwards.

—Amy Tan

*I*n September 1996, after *Simple Abundance* had been No. 1 on the *New York Times* best-seller list for six months, it was published in England, where reviewing books in the inspiration genre is often viewed as an exercise in humorous writing or blood sport. "Bad hair, overdrafts, dirty floors—don't let them get you down, let them enrich you" was some of the derision meted out to *Simple Abundance*. One particularly nasty and unscrupulous hack (who had the gall to pretend he'd met and interviewed me) wrote something that inadvertently not only became the banner headline for my book in Europe, but it also set me on the search for my House of Belonging. "Sarah Ban Breathnach might be described as the Isaac Newton of the simplicity movement," he wise-cracked. At a cocktail party this banter might have sounded hilarious; in print it became high praise.

How I roared with laughter when I read that. This unintentional compliment was not only a hoot but a generous gift. No longer was it necessary for me to dream about winning the Pulitzer or Nobel Prize; a magnificent obituary was guaranteed. My foreign publishers were particularly thrilled and used the line with glee in their publicity campaigns. *"Sarah Ban Breathnach puo essere paragonata all'Isaac Newton del movimento della semplicita...,"* my Italian publishers proudly boasted. I loved it.

Naturally, after this cosmic comparison, I developed a mad, passionate crush on Sir Isaac Newton, as one does, and wanted to know everything about him. What I learned intrigued and fascinated me; the man wasn't only the first modern scientist, but he was a mystic after my own heart.

The following summer, while casually flipping through an English newspaper "coincidentally" discarded in an airport waiting lounge, I discovered that a cottage that had previously been Sir Isaac Newton's private chapel was for sale. Good Heavens! How often did this happen? Maybe once in several lifetimes. I had to return to New York but immediately sent for details.

A month later, the mystical chain of chance continued when *People* magazine unexpectedly sent me to London as a special correspondent covering Princess Diana's funeral. And so I extended my stay a couple of days and traveled to what seemed to me to be the wilds of rural England, *just* to take a look.

CHANGING PLACES

It was a love like a chord from Bach, of such pure gravity.

—Nina Cassian

Just one look, that's all it took. Just one look, and the earth tilted on its axis. Wham! Bam! "Thank you, Madam," the estate agent said, smiling broadly.

I fell truly, madly, deeply. Swooned, I seem to recall, with the same witless intensity usually reserved for unsuitable men. "Who ever loved, that loved not at first sight?" the 16th-century English playwright Christopher Marlowe wondered and rightly so.

The facts are these: I was newly separated and shaky after my long-standing marriage had ended abruptly; I didn't know a soul in England. I gave no thought to the life changes this love affair would trigger. I *didn't* call my best friend to ask for advice. What *does* that tell you?

Why am I doing this? I asked the "Voice" urging me to buy the cottage, then and there.

"It will all be revealed in the By-and-By..."

There's more. The cottage was 900 years old and only had two rooms. Recalling the exact moment my common sense went south—from the sublime to the ridiculous in a fleeting glance—only one word comes to mind: Home. (*Certifiable* could be another, but unfortunately this clarity comes only with hindsight.)

THE LOOK OF LOVE

Put all your eggs in one basket and—WATCH THAT BASKET!

—Mark Twain

I have always been touched by the story of the American writer Samuel Clemens, who in 1874 moved into his dream house—an imposing, nineteen-room, red brick, Gothic mansion in Hartford, Connecticut—with his wife and three daughters. Over the next two decades, Sam and Livy decorated, renovated, and lavished so much time, creative energy, emotion, and money on their house it forced him into bankruptcy. Luckily for us, Clemens solved his financial problems and continued to decorate by writing books under the pseudonym Mark Twain. But that building was not just a house; it was their *home*—their sacred partner—in their union with Life. In a letter to a friend in 1896, Clemens described their House of Belonging this way:

To us, our house was not insentient matter—it had a heart and a soul, and eyes to see us with; and approvals and solicitudes and deep sympathies; it was of us, and we were in its confidence and lived in its grace and in the peace of its benedictions. We never came home from an absence that its face did not light up and speak out its eloquent welcome—and we could not enter it unmoved.

I can't explain my love for Newton's Chapel any better. From the moment I opened the garden gate, a strange enchantment took hold. "Enchanted places have the power to change us, to germinate and nurture that tiny seed of happiness … that each of us have kept so carefully concealed," the English writer Alexandra Campbell reveals in her novel *Remember This*. I felt as if I belonged here. All my life, I've never felt as if I belonged *anywhere*; my harried heart was possessed by a mysterious "holy longing" that never seemed to be satisfied. But here, in the garden of this tiny ivory stone cottage with its huge, ancient apple tree, heavily laden with reddening and ripening orbs, I felt that there couldn't possibly be anyplace else more exquisite—nothing more to be desired. The warmth of the September afternoon made the earth fragrant, yeasty, and fruity; bees flitted among the drooping pink hollyhocks. Wasps droned over sweetly decaying apples on the ground, drunk in delight. Doves cooed from the top of the red-peaked tile roof. Across the meadow, sheep grazed on a green hill bordered by hedgerows of blackberries.

My search for True Love was over.

ON HOLY GROUND

I understood. I have understood. I do understand.

—Sir Isaac Newton

Inside Newton's Chapel, the stillness was so luxurious, it took my breath away. The silence was lyrical; the atmosphere sensuous; the very air was intoxicating, an aura that was simultaneously serene and exhilarating. Delicious goose bumps ran up and down my spine; I wanted to giggle;

the next moment, I wanted to cry with relief. It also felt sacred; I knew I was standing on holy ground. The old dark wooden beams supporting the roof looked as sturdy as the day they were hoisted sometime in the 12th century; the plaster walls were five feet thick; and in one room stood a partially exposed but completely intact Norman arch twelve feet high. I rubbed my hand slightly against the grainy stone, and a hush soothed my heart and summarily dismissed my head from the negotiations. A palpable awe came over me; I was draped in a mantle of reverence as soft as cashmere. I felt so safe, so loved, so protected. So chosen. I knew I had been led there, step by step, by some mysterious grace. I knew that I had come home.

"It is no exaggeration to say that almost everything we do in the modern world is based on Sir Isaac Newton's enormous scientific achievements—but he was not the pure scientist of lore," Michael White tells us in his riveting biography, *Isaac Newton: The Last Sorcerer*. "Unknown to all but a few, Newton was a practicing alchemist who dabbled with the occult. He did not discover gravity by watching an apple fall—in reality, Newton's great theories were grasped within the charred base of the crucible and the alchemist's fire. Nor was Newton the idealistic puritan that he has always been seen as, but a tortured, obsessive character who risked his health in a ceaseless quest for an understanding of the universe through whatever means at his disposal."

These means included studying the Bible for divination instead of dogma, the practice of natural magic, reliance on

astrology and numerology when he conducted mathemati-
cal experiments, and most of all, attempting to unravel
Divine secrets, from the infinite to the infinitesimal, through
alchemy. Newton looked upon all of creation as a cosmic
riddle, with clues hidden in plain view by God—the colors
of a rainbow, the fall of an apple, the pull of the tides. But
alchemy was considered by the Church to be the darkest sin
and most dangerous magical practice; this process could
transform matter—for example, a base metal such as iron,
into gold—and the pursuit of this arcane knowledge was
absolutely forbidden. Although a deeply spiritual man,
Newton was not religious and withdrew from society for
long periods of time, leading a lonely, hidden existence. He
feared that if his practice of alchemy and passion for magic
were discovered, it would discredit his scientific contribu-
tions. In fact, so thorough was his subterfuge that it was only
in 1932 when his private, encrypted jottings—thought to be
of no value to his scientific papers—were auctioned off that
his secret was revealed. And what a secret it was!

I sensed that the Chapel was where he got away from the
experiments he conducted in his manor house just down the
lane; here in his sacred, clandestine bolt hole, Sir Isaac
Newton came to think, meditate, ruminate, listen, and
above all, find peace. The Chapel was private, locked; no one
could enter without his permission. Here was where Heaven
came down to Earth for private tutorials with the man who
would give the world an understanding of the Cosmos. The
Chapel was Newton's true sanctuary. Now nearly 350 years

later, Heaven was not only opening the door for me, but was handing me the key! The thought filled me with astonishment. It was as if I were applying for a mystical, magical apprenticeship.

I wondered: If I remained here could I unravel my own cosmic mystery? Could I finally understand who I was and what was my place in the world?

HEARTWORK

Now for some heartwork.

—Rainer Maria Rilke

*I*n the beginning, *Simple Abundance* wasn't meant to be a book at all. It was a deeply personal, practical, creative, and spiritual process I originated to help me discover what truly mattered most in my life. I called it my "heartwork." *Simple Abundance* was an experiment with Life because my version of it felt out of control. At that time, like fifty million other working mothers, life had become an out-of-body experience for me. I was rushing from one obligation to the next so fast that my spirit felt as if it was constantly sprinting to catch up with me, which it finally did when I collapsed into bed. Mornings became major sources of dread; my first conscious breath was a sigh; my awaking thought only a question: How could I make it through the day? I didn't have a moment to myself, or a moment's peace. I felt my real job wasn't writer, wife, or mother, but magician, for I became brilliant at sleight of hand and a mistress of smoke and mirrors.

This was in 1991 when the downturn in the economy shocked America into a scarcity syndrome. Gone were the padded shoulders and excesses of the eighties, replaced by sackcloth and ashes. It wasn't quite the Great Depression, but who knew what tomorrow might bring? As American President Harry Truman explained it: "It's a recession when your neighbor loses his job; it's a depression when you lose yours." Call it what you want to, but there was doom and gloom everywhere—an absolute pandemic of lack. Americans were downshifting out of necessity, and we didn't like it one bit.

Like everyone else, the more I focused on lack, the more depressed and worried I became; the more depressed and worried I'd wake up, the more I focused on what was lacking in my life all day. Worries about money followed me around like a dark, menacing shadow. It was a vicious, soul-crushing cycle. Of course, I never whined about it to anyone else, but I constantly complained to myself and to Spirit. I was such an angry, envious woman. One morning I woke up and just couldn't take the sound of my own kvetching anymore, so my soul said, "That's it, Sarah. I don't want to hear another word about what's missing from your life. I want you to sit down at this table and not get up until you give me over 100 reasons you're *grateful* for the gift of your life, exactly as it is now."

Six hours and as many pots of tea later, I'd come up with a master list of my life's overlooked blessings. I was so humbled and ashamed, for I realized that, indeed, I was a woman very rich in blessings; what I was experiencing was a temporary cash flow problem. The grace of Gratitude seemed to knock at the door and whispered, "I can help you get your life back on track."

The 13th-century German mystic Meister Eckhart tells us that if the only prayer you ever say in your life is "Thank you" it will be enough. I discovered just how right he was. So I started saying "thank you" for all the little pleasant things that would happen in the course of a day: finding a parking space when I was late for a meeting; the peonies which bloomed early just when I needed to make a bouquet; the cozy texture of a favorite sweater; the delicious aroma that filled the house when I was simmering spaghetti sauce; an extra hour in bed because of a snow day. Because gratitude was such a new practice for me, I started writing down five things for which I was grateful each day; I didn't want to ever forget again.

Within two months of keeping a Gratitude Journal, I was a completely different woman. Nothing had occurred to change my circumstances as far as money was concerned, but every day I noticed more moments of contentment than distress. I *knew* that I was onto something and began writing *Simple Abundance*. Toni Morrison said, "If there is a book you really want to read, but it hasn't been written yet, then you must write it." I followed her advice. It would take me four years to complete, and during that time it was rejected 30 times for not being "commercial enough."

There really is no bigger thrill than doing what the world says can't be done. By the time I was standing in Newton's cottage, *Simple Abundance* had sold scads of copies and been translated into myriad languages, and I had all the world's golden gifts lying at my Manolo Blahnik-clad feet. I was much sought after and fussed over, made to feel important and grand, which, admittedly, was quite fabulous. I had enough money to establish the Simple Abundance Charitable Trust (which supports nonprofit causes through my royalties), pay for my daughter's college education, and travel on the Concorde. But in my private life, I was alone, living as singularly as Newton.

Inevitably, the larger my public persona grew, the smaller my circle of intimates became. Isolation is one of celebrity's more uncomfortable footnotes. And while acclaim, awards, and applause are often very agreeable fellows to have a drink with, their conversation rarely moves past small talk. As Coco Chanel so succinctly put it: "That's what fame is: *solitude.*"

Initially I'd been very flattered by all the attention. However, after a couple of frenzied years, I was over-whelmed and, frankly, exhausted by the sheer volume of requests: to speak, give money, franchise my name, extend the *Simple Abundance* brand, sit on boards of directors, but most of all, write more books—as fast as possible.

I'd received more than 40,000 letters thanking me for writing *Simple Abundance*; many women shared their poignant stories and told me how the book had helped them through great difficulty, struggle, and sorrow. I was as dazed as I was deeply moved to hear from readers in such an inti-mate way, and I did my best to give every letter personal attention. However, I was also bewildered by the world's impression of just who Sarah Ban Breathnach was, and increasingly the public image of the woman who wrote *Simple Abundance* began to restrict my life in a disturbing way. At book signings some women would seem dismayed that I wore high heels and red nail polish and they would tell me so. *"That's not what I expected you to look like."* One woman went so far as to exclaim: *"Oh,* **you** *can't be my Sarah. My Sarah doesn't look like you!"* I asked her what "her" Sarah looked like and she told me she wore Laura Ashley and Birkenstocks!

So while aspects of being a celebrity were intoxicating, and I had no problem depositing those royalty checks, keeping up the public persona of "SBB" became debilitating. I always loved Marilyn Monroe's observation that people think fame gives fans "some kind of privilege to walk up to you and say anything to you, of any kind of nature—and it won't hurt your feelings." When my marriage ended I experienced not only shock and heartbreak but a deep sense of shame and embarrassment. I went to great lengths to keep it quiet for as long as I could, believing, misguidedly, that somehow I'd let my fans down. *Simple Abundance* had become more than a best seller; it had grown into a myth about living perfectly. It was also becoming too, too much.

The last time I looked, I'd been driving the car pool, changing the kitty litter, and waiting for the chopped meat to defrost in the microwave so I could make meat loaf. Now I was searching for solace after the wrenching weekend of reporting on Princess Diana's funeral for *People* magazine. I'd covered it from Hyde Park where hundreds of thousands of people slept, wept, and waited for the funeral cortege to move past them. Swept along by the crowds and feeling less a member of the media than a mourner among her masses, there wasn't a doubt in my mind that this glorious woman—so adored and admired for her beauty, style, devotion, sense of honor, conviction, and compassion—was deeply and passionately loved by the world. But it wasn't the world's love that she craved. She wanted her Happily Ever After. Like you, like me. Diana was searching for her House of Belonging, and it wasn't the House of Windsor.

As I stood in Newton's Chapel, my past and future intersected. I knew I didn't ever want to leave because when I did I would be facing more expectations, deadlines, obligations, and responsibilities. I knew that the only way I could part from this sacred place was if I also *knew* I'd be coming back. I remembered what Willa Cather said: "One cannot divine nor forecast the conditions that will make happiness. One only stumbles upon them by chance, in a lucky hour, at the world's end somewhere, and holds fast to the days, as to fortune or fame." I desperately wanted to believe her, so I made an offer on the spot to buy Newton's Chapel. But I wouldn't be holding onto fortune or fame because, in truth, I was running away from them just as fast as my leopard-skin stilettos could manage.

THE ULTIMATE AMBITION

To be happy at home is the ultimate result of all ambition.

—Samuel Johnson

"There is nothing stranger than success. The moment the creature arrives, it subtly alters the very work we did to become successful in the first place," the modern English poet David Whyte ponders in his powerful, provocative, and consoling book, *Crossing the Unknown Sea: Work as a Pilgrimage of Identity.* I'm a great admirer of his work. A stanza of Whyte's exquisite poem "The House of Belonging," which embodies this book's theme, is stenciled on the upstairs landing of my house where I see it every day. Still, it's poignant how something so meaningful to us can become diminished through familiarity, even to the point of becoming unrecognizable. I don't think familiarity breeds as much contempt as it does indifference. Usually I'm dashing up the stairs at full throttle and don't notice the words; I probably only absorb the poem's meaning when I'm giving a friend a tour of the house and we both stop to read it together.

My husband pokes his head around the office door to tell me he heard on the radio that 41 percent of women *worldwide* covet my job.

"And what job is that exactly?"

"Writing. Best-selling books."

This news is meant to cheer me up. But it doesn't, because with all the work I've done these last ten years there hasn't been much time left over for musing, meditating, and meandering, which I'm always telling you to do more often. Antiquing, puttering, arranging flowers, sorting through old makeup, repotting a plant, tacking charming French shelf tape in the linen closet, going horseback riding, making an apple and rhubarb pie, rearranging my spice cabinet. You'd think to watch me constantly at the computer that I've forgotten that I gave millions of women permission to discover what makes them happy and then do it. But I haven't forgotten. Someone has to write the permission note.

"We shape our work, and then, not surprisingly, we are shaped again by the work we have done," David Whyte explains. "Sometimes to our distress, we find ourselves in a place where the work suddenly seems to be doing all the shaping, where we do not seem able to lift ourselves out of the mud of our own making, where we do not feel able to shape ourselves at all."

AFTER THE FALL

> *Domestic happiness, thou only bliss*
> *Of Paradise that has survived the fall!*
>
> —William Cowper

For half my life I've been writing about pursuing domestic bliss, while actually achieving very little of it myself. If it sounds like I'm complaining, I am. But I'm doing so to make a point. I can't be the only woman worn to a raveling. I know you are too. The world has changed so dramatically in the last decade since *Simple Abundance* was published; at times it feels as if we've barely survived the Fall from grace. The task of getting through the day with all our loved ones accounted for drains our energy, depletes our sense of security, and diminishes our capacity for happiness, leaving us feeling exhausted and vulnerable. Nearly every day we're inundated with a new reason to be scared—if it's not a terrorist alert, it's fears about bird flu or Yellowstone National Park blowing up. As Dorothy Parker so succinctly asked, "What fresh hell is this?"

Let's take a fresh look at a word that saps our strength so often:

Scared

"What difference do it make if the thing you scared of is real or not?" wonders Toni Morrison. Fair enough question. Women have always known how to comfort the fears of others; we just don't remember to use the same tender, loving tactics on ourselves. So the next time you feel a random panic attack starting, take a deep breath, and transpose the *"a"* and the *"c"* in "scared" and you'll find not only another word but a world of difference. You'll uncover the

Sacred

Doesn't that make you feel better already? It works for me, every time. I'd be willing to bet the house that your sacred, like mine, is very close—the walls surrounding you or the floorboards supporting you, even if they need a good scrub. The best definition I ever heard of fear is "false evidence appearing real." When I'm anxious I notice that my fears seem to be speculative future-tense marauders. *Will there be enough? What will I do? How will I cope?* The best way I know to disarm such fear is by keeping a Gratitude Journal. A Gratitude Journal is a polite, daily thank-you note to the Universe—and a reminder to yourself of the very real blessings you have now. In this moment. You know how insulted you are after you've knocked yourself out for your kids and all you get in return is surly silence. What am I raising, you probably wonder, a bunch of brats? Well, an ancient spiritual axiom teaches us, "As below, so above."

Because you're not spoiled rotten, at the end of every day you write down five things or moments you experienced for which to be thankful. Small pauses that brought a smile or a sense of relief during the day. The kindness of somebody holding your place in the post office line when you have a lot of packages to get from the car. The plumber showing up on time. Fitting into last summer's shorts. A hug from a friend. A fortune cookie with just the right message. Saying no to the bake sale without guilt. Easily switching carpooling days. Getting an extension on the deadline. Better yet, meeting the deadline. Phew!

We think it's the big moments that define our lives—the promotion, the new baby, the renovated kitchen, the wedding. But the narrative of our lives is written in the small, the simple, and the common. The overlooked. The discarded. The reclaimed. Life is not made up of minutes, hours, days, weeks, months, or years, but of moments. You must experience each one before you can appreciate it.

Whether you're chopping carrots, shampooing your hair, writing a memo, making love, talking on the telephone, walking the dog, or eating an apple, savor those sensations involved. All of these moments, whether happy, routine, or even painful, are Life's heartbeats.

Here's my favorite Gratitude Journal story: I was invited to teach a *Simple Abundance* workshop at the Disney Institute in Orlando, and my daughter's long-promised, long-awaited trip to Disney World arrived—all expenses paid. One day when I was not teaching, I joined Katie and her dad. But the day was cut short by a sudden thunderstorm and it took several hours for us to make our way back to our hotel. By the time we did, we were all drenched to the skin and chilled to the bone. After taking hot showers and changing into dry clothes, we went down to the little restaurant in the hotel for a pizza supper. The contented feeling of being warm and dry and happy together was so palpable that they were the first "gifts" I jotted down in my Gratitude Journal that night. Months later I was flipping through my journal and to my great astonishment saw another entry for that day: *Simple Abundance* hit *USA Today*'s best-seller list for the first time! You would think that this achievement would have been the first on my list, but it wasn't, because I'd learned to appreciate the precious but fleeting moments in my life—morsels of contentment that truly do make a difference in how you feel, day in, day out. Writing these moments down transforms gratitude from a spiritual sensibility to personal knowledge, experience you can really trust.

INTERIOR VISION

Your vision will become clear only when you can look into your heart. Who looks outside, dreams; who looks inside, awakes.

—Carl Jung

Those of you who are already familiar (and grateful) for the miracle of harnessing the power of the Universe with just two little words—"Thank you"—might like this new approach with your Gratitude Journal. As long as you're working on the moving on process, I'd like you to focus your concentration on your House of Belonging. We're going to start giving thanks for five things that are already perfect with the home you're living in at the moment. Do you have a dishwasher or clothes dryer? Right there are two reasons to be grateful, which you remember pretty quickly when either of them goes on the fritz. What about a fabulously comfortable chair? A room with a view? A tub deep enough to submerge your shoulders under warm, fragrant bubbles? You get the idea. No complaints now. (We'll deal with those in another way.) Right now, I just want you to take an interior inventory in order to praise your home. As Elsie de Wolfe believed, and you will soon, "There never has been a house so bad that it couldn't be made over into something worthwhile."

BEING HOME

Peace—that was the other name for home.

—Kathleen Norris

Maybe you're contentedly married or happily part-nered; maybe you're living alone for the first time (or for the first time in many years) either by chance or choice; maybe you're exploring the joys and growing pains of re-wedded bliss; maybe you're living with different generations under one roof or making life up as you go along with a family of friends. But whatever your living arrangements might be, with children or without, at this time in all our lives, there should be no more embarrassment or reluctance to admit we're besotted with an idea as old as time: Being Home.

"If a hungry friend came and knocked at your door on a cold night, you would graciously welcome her in, sit her by the fire, help her shed her wet, clumsy clothes. You'd give her a blanket to wrap herself in and a cup of hot soup to warm and nourish herself. Then, when she was rested, well fed and comfortable, her story might emerge," Elizabeth Murray reminds us in her glorious book, *Cultivating Sacred Space*. "Your hospitality, your love and acceptance would soothe your friend, and the soft warm light of your hearth would pull her out of her dark night. This is what our soul asks us to do for ourselves every night when we cross the threshold to the hearth of our homes."

TRUTH OR DARE

Talent is helpful in writing, but guts are absolutely necessary.

—Jessamyn West

For centuries young women have learned how to run a home, how to cook, and how to raise a family by tying themselves to their mothers' or grandmothers' apron strings. "When they wanted to make their menfolk feel how important they were, our great-grandmothers were fond of quoting 'the hand that rocks the cradle rules the world,' " the English novelist Mary Dunn wrote in an essay for young women, *The Queen Was in the Kitchen,* published in 1950. "At the present moment—and I expect conditions will be much the same when you grow up—there doesn't seem to be much time for cradle rocking, because the cradle-rocker is too busy running the house and thinking about or preparing the next meal. Though, of course, babies are just as important to-day as ever they were, it would be more true to say it is the hand that peels the potatoes, fries the onions a beautiful golden brown, ices the birthday cake, folds the omelet, or makes a dish out of almost nothing at all that rules the world."

She goes on to ask her young English readers to "think of America. You must have seen films with a kitchen queen. The slim, attractive wife—or even a plump, attractive one— in the most ravishing little apron, pulling pans out of ovens, dishing up creamy sweets, or merely opening refrigerator doors in one of those dazzling kitchens with built-in cupboards everywhere, spotless sinks, and rows of gleaming aluminum saucepans. I don't know about you, but I always feel disappointed when the kitchen queen takes off her apron, smooths down her dress, and goes to join her guests in the living room. Of course, she still looks ravishing, with never a hair out of place, but somehow in the living room she loses her crown as it were, and becomes an ordinary person again. Perhaps, if you have never been to America, you think you would have been looking at a fancy world and America isn't like that. You would be wrong. Most American kitchens are like that and nearly all American girls really are splendid cooks, and really do whisk up superb meals and appear five minutes later in their living rooms looking too glamorous to be true."

Unfortunately, this American girl wasn't raised that way. Kitchen queen is the fantasy to which I continue to aspire when I grow up; you should see my vintage apron collection. But the sorry truth is I never *even* learned to boil an egg until I left home. Nonetheless, when I was a senior in high school I won a Betty Crocker "Homemaker of Tomorrow" award. This greatly perplexed and amused the nuns who taught me, considering that Home Ec was not even part of our curriculum. It also floored my mother, who knew the state of my bedroom and her continuous struggle to get me to clean it. But I had won the contest—based on an essay and *not* a bake-off—by writing about the importance of homemaking as an endangered calling. I guess coming events do cast their shadows beforehand. This was in 1965 when the rumblings of the feminist movement were starting to be heard across the land. In the mid-'60s you didn't prepare your daughter for life by teaching her to make a bed, sort laundry, organize a closet, or make a casserole. Instead, many mothers handed out copies of *The Feminine Mystique* after they had finished reading it themselves.

Now four decades later, women know how to start online auction businesses, launch banks and new magazines, walk in space, trade securities on Wall Street, close million-dollar movie deals, get elected to national office, anchor the nightly news, write Supreme Court decisions, conduct American diplomacy, and win Nobel Prizes. Women can create, innovate, delegate, negotiate, and beat the boys with a smile. But we're also running to the grocery store on our way home from work, washing the laundry when everyone in the family has run out of clothes to wear, and searching for a place to sit down comfortably at the end of a long day in the midst of complete and utter pandemonium (coincidentally, the English poet John Milton's name for the capital of hell in *Paradise Lost*).

Does any of this sound remotely familiar? Okay. Truth or dare time: How many women do you know who run successful businesses but don't have a clue how to run their own households competently? Well, I won't tell, if you won't. But here's a hint: Wisteria Lane isn't the only street with desperate housewives.

"If we had a feminism that caused us to get out of the house," asks the French Canadian philosopher Ginette Paris, "is there not also room for feminism that would bring us back home so that our homes would reflect ourselves and would once more have soul?"

Hold that thought.

WHAT'S IN A NAME

Naming is a difficult and time-consuming process; it concerns essences, and it means power. But on wild nights who can call you home? Only the one who knows your name.

—Jeanette Winterson

*E*mily Dickinson believed *Home* was another name for God. Helen Keller described God as the "Light in my darkness, the Voice in my silence." The 13th-century mystic Julian of Norwich told her novitiates, "God is our clothing that wraps, clasps, and encloses us." Every time I slip into my beloved comfy robe at the end of a long, harrowing day, I remember how right she was.

In the Hebrew tradition, so holy and hidden is the Almighty's identity that the proper name of God cannot be pronounced. But in English it is written as four sacred letters—YHWH—representing the past, present, and future tense of the verb *to be*. God told Moses to call on the great "I AM," and when Moses did, the seas parted and his people were fed daily while wandering in the wilderness for forty years. Many of them probably looked up to the sky calling their God *Manna*, the name of the heavenly substance that arrived each morning and kept them alive. Interestingly, manna could not be hoarded and saved for the next day; it turned rancid and inedible. So does our understanding of spirituality need to be kept fresh. We need to rediscover ways to acknowledge the generosity of Spirit by recognizing the mystical in the mundane. Those readers familiar with my work know that my credo is that the sacred is found in our ordinary moments. Everyday life is the prayer. If you have followed the *Simple Abundance* path and found fulfillment, then we share the belief that women pray not just on their knees but with every breath, with every heartbeat, with every smile, sigh, tear, and laugh. We know it *does* matter how we braid her hair, pack his lunch, send them on their way, greet their return, make suggestions, change the contract, return the phone call, pass the pasta, pour the wine, clean the house, listen to a friend, visit her in a nursing home, change the sheets, check for monsters under the bed. We know it all matters and that grace is when you both can savor the small things—and not sweat the big ones.

Every woman who believes in God calls the Holy One by a particular name; those with no faith or one different from yours or mine will choose another word to describe God. In my books I often use the word *Spirit* for God because I do not want to impose on my readers my own expanding view of Divinity. The artist and writer Julia Cameron, who gave the world the brilliant *The Artist's Way,* believes in a festive and creative God, and I agree. "After all, Somebody had an awfully good time making hibiscus blossoms, red clay cliffs, rivers, starfish, pinecones, coral snakes and stars," she notes in *The Vein of Gold: A Journey to Your Creative Heart.* "In our culture, God is so often thought of in terms of Calvinist austerity and renunciation that we forget there was clearly a godly glee in creative excess, an artist in love with the materials themselves."

For those uncomfortable with the idea of an expansive, abundant Divinity, Julia Cameron suggests thinking of God as "good orderly direction," which is a great way to re-imagine Spirit. "But, ultimately we all get the God we believe in [which is why] it behooves us to be very conscious of which god we believe in and invoke."

The House of Belonging is part of the expansive Celtic spiritual tradition which is ebullient and exuberant in its all embracing nature of Divinity. As Caitlin Matthews tells us in her luminous *Celtic Devotional: Daily Prayers and Blessings,* Celtic spirituality has many exquisite and descriptive names for Divinity, all of which honor the sacred in the ordinary: *Source of All Mystery, Gate of Gladness, Mother of Memory, Piercer of Doubt, Kindler of Hope, Keeper of Good Cheer, Ever Present Provider, Compassionate Listener, Guardian of the Hearth, Only Source, Ancient Dream, Glad Giver, Weaver of Wonder, Revelation of Evening, Teller of Tales, and Queen of Quietness,* among many others.

"Mystics and poets of all eras and spiritualities have called upon the Divine according to the needs of their hearts; as rock, door, tree, ground of knowledge; as mother, father, sister, brother, friend, beloved; as keeper, creator, watcher, restorer, and giver of hope," she tells us. "Mystics are poets of the spirit who speak with the metaphor of delight. But every living person is also a potential mystic with an immediate and spontaneous response to the wonder of the universe."

I believe that all women are inherently mystical, that being able to recognize the essence of what is sacred is a part of what it means to be feminine. Women are endowed not with just five senses, but with seven. Through caring for your home as a prayer in progress you can rediscover not only sight, sound, scent, taste, and touch in your daily round, but you also come to cherish your sixth sense of "knowing"—a woman's intuitive sense—and the seventh sense of "wonder"—your sense of rapture and reverence.

Wonder is that extravagant state of bliss induced by something new—the strange, astonishing, mysterious, and the unexpected. I believe this bliss is part of creating your House of Belonging. "Eden is that old-fashioned House we dwell in every day," Emily Dickinson reminds us. May we all be as truly awake to this grace.

As you read this book, please be open to the vastness of the Divine and the limits of language, for I shall use many different ways to express the concept of Spirit as we make our daily round through the rooms of the House of Belonging. Some of these names may surprise you. Here's a hint: If you come across a word beginning with a capital letter, I am trying to describe, however feebly, an aspect of Divinity that has comforted, sustained, and delighted me. Personally, in the course of a day I may invoke several in my own devotional path. When I'm writing, I ask the Great Creator to inspire me and keep me at it; if I'm hurting, I invoke the help of the Gentle Healer; if the unexpected blessing of a boisterous guffaw pierces through my earnestness, I have Milady of the Laugh to thank; when I'm fretful and worn to a raveling, I turn my exhaustion over to my beloved Sower of Sleep. "I understand why one wants to know the names of what [she] loves," the writer Jessamyn West explains. "Naming is a kind of possessing, of caressing and fondling." Throughout this book, I shall be sharing with you some of my own personal meditations invoked as I have sought to create my own House of Belonging. May you find them a blessing and a door that's been left slightly ajar. Just knock and you'll be welcomed in, dearest Reader.

DO TRY THIS AT HOME:
A SCRAPBOOK NAMED DESIRE

Desire is prayer.
—Terry McMillan

Whether a woman is single, divorced, or married, there's no passion as perfect as the dream house she will someday inhabit; no romantic obsession as consuming as her home's beautiful décor; and no illusion as seductive as the fanciful notion that once she crosses the threshold, she'll stay there forever.

From the scented linen closet to the built-in kitchen pantry, from the window seat, plump with needlepoint pillows, to the rose-covered arbor leading to the backyard, each nook and cranny of this fantasy has been lovingly imagined since we were little girls "playing house." No doubt, the magic spell was cast when Mother draped a blanket over the dining room chairs and we crawled underneath to put our dollies to bed.

"Even though your dream house is at the end of a long, long road, your head may be buzzing with plans for that home you will have someday. Already you probably have a stack of clippings, sketches and what not—ideas you want to remember for your own house," Elinor Hillyer reassured the young woman who purchased *Mademoiselle's Home Planning Scrapbook* in 1946. "You can't keep all those house plans in your head—keep them in here."

The scrapbook is 12x15 inches, silver-gray cardboard, spiral bound with big envelopes—one for every room—to stash paper dreams. I'm amazed by the synchronicity between it and my own *Simple Abundance Illustrated Discovery Journal* published 50 years later, which was also a spiral bound journal with envelopes. But I've just come across this treasure. Like many women, I adore antiquing. Somehow sifting through the domestic shards of those who no longer can bear witness to life's glorious mystery helps me ransom, reclaim, and redeem what is truly precious in my own.

Unfortunately, I'm stumped by Elinor Hillyer's first rule for successful dream house planning. *"Have a fair picture in mind of the kind of home you want and the kind of life you and your young man want to build for yourselves."* To be perfectly honest, I created the first *Illustrated Discovery Journal*, my own, as a personal insight tool because I couldn't visualize the life or house I wanted to live it in.

However, I sure know what I'd like to fill the dream house with. Everything! Pink-and-black-striped silk pillows, red refrigerator, pale blue cast iron pots, a flat television screen that folds into a smart rattan armoire at the foot of my king-size canopy bed, stereo speakers without wires… I could go on, but I'll restrain myself.

Just last night, I embellished this fantasy and maybe you did, too, by flipping through the latest magazines, ripping out this month's desires to be tossed into my bulging Dream House Archive. I've been doing this for 25 years and it's grown so vast, it really should be called the Dream House Annex. During that time, my dream house has run the gamut from a Victorian gingerbread to a Frank Lloyd Wright prairie manse to a French chateau surrounded by a moat. What fascinates me is that while the physical design of my dream house alters, the Dream House Archive's expansion remains constant—a potent and poignant labyrinth of yearning. A persuasive palliative too. My escape addiction of choice any time of day is a glossy home shelter magazine. Just as I can't read a book without a yellow highlighter, I can't read a magazine without ripping the pages out. I have to sit on my hands in waiting rooms.

In many respects my Dream House Archive is a psychic waiting room, a repository of secret despair as well as desire.

Whenever I catch a glimpse of the Dream House Archive, which now occupies prime shelf space in my office, it makes me wince; so many desires for physical things. The poet Wallace Stevens believed that the "greatest poverty" is "to feel that one's desire is too difficult to tell from despair."

I'm at the site of my soul, right now, rustling the layers of clippings at random like raffle tickets, plunging deep to see what I so fervently wished for once upon a time; as adorable as this white changing table/dresser stenciled in pink roses is, it's no longer needed in my daughter's bedroom. That's because she's 23 and has her own Los Angeles apartment. But it certainly would be a dream come true if I had a kidney-shaped dressing table with a dust ruffle in pink taffeta and a comfortable chair to sit down upon in order to perform my *maquillage* in peace. While I'm at it, I'd love a large oval mirror, ample natural light, and convenient electrical outlets. At present, I stand in a tiny bathroom using a mirror propped against the window with my makeup strewn all over the top of the toilet.

Many women keep Dream Files. Do you? The writer and editor-in-chief of *House & Garden*, Dominique Browning, speaks of her love for this feminine ritual which she does "in a spirit of hope. Someday I'll need all these pictures to communicate what it is that I see, in my mind's eye, to whoever will help me build my dream house."

Perhaps that's true, but something tells me that most women's Dream Files are more tinged with relinquishment and resignation than hope. Somehow we think that by consigning our desires to the great void of *Someday*, whether it's a basket, box, or fabric-covered file, we're another step closer to fulfilling them. I hate to be the one to tell you this, because I've always been a great gal for ripping, clipping, and delayed gratification, but we're deluding ourselves.

"Unfulfilled desires are dangerous forces," the Victorian educator Sarah Tarleton Colvin warns us. In order for a desire to remain unfulfilled, it must be continuously unacknowledged; better yet, hide it so cunningly in plain view, like a file basket (or five), and in a decade maybe you'll forget you were aroused in the first place; in two decades, the moment, as they say, will have passed.

Unless the despair starts to smolder. There are some perfectly reasonable desires we ignore at our sanity's peril. Take my dressing table fantasy. While it sounds like I'm coveting a confection worthy of Madame Pompadour, lift the pink taffeta skirt of this longing and you'll discover what my soul is really craving is space, light, and order, which are basic needs in any room, in any house. I bet I can deconstruct what you think are your frivolous, wanton, extravagant, spendthrift desires pretty quickly too, but better yet, I'm going to show you how to do so yourself.

It's been about 50 years since one of the most famous cases of spontaneous human combustion was reported. It was a

Philadelphia housewife in 1957. Usually the victims are women. Medical investigators still don't know why someone suddenly bursts into flames, like a log consumed from within, without burning anything else surrounding it. Ask any woman who keeps a Dream House file bursting with clippings so old that her desires are tattered yellowed scraps, brown at the edges, and spontaneous combustion will no longer remain an unsolved mystery.

So here's what we're going to do. We're going to stop procrastinating about getting what we want out of life and get rid of the Dream House file. No more dreams on hold. "Someday" is as big a malarkey as "mañana." Making dreams come true—and I've been blessed to see more than a few of mine materialize—requires passion, persistence, and planning, not passive detachment. Time to move on. "Action is the antidote to despair," Joan Baez tells us.

First, I want you to sift and sort through that Dream House file, if you have one, keeping only those images that still make your heart beat faster. Get rid of the rest.

Now I want you to walk through your house and play "candid camera," taking snapshots of each room, as well as closets, cupboards, hallways, and hideaways, *just as they are at this moment.* Yes, this is really scary. But remember that the sacred is hidden behind this seemingly pointless exercise. I promise.

While you're information-gathering, see if you can't find photographs from as many of your previous homes as possible. It would be great if you had a picture of your first home.

Finally, go to an art supply store and get the largest spiral-bound artist's notebook you can find (at least 11x14 inches); sharp scissors, glue sticks, colored pencils (the watercolor ones are wonderful; after you draw you can go over your work with water on a paintbrush and voila!—you're a painter), and two dozen large mailing envelopes.

We're going to create *The House of Belonging Companion*. Just as the Gratitude Journal will offer you many glimmers of all that's right about your home and the deep awareness of the "simple abundance" that surrounds you daily, *The House of Belonging Companion*—your scrapbook named desire— accelerates the unfolding of your Home Making talents through pure intuition and imagination—the secret language of your heart and soul.

If you're familiar with the *Illustrated Discovery Journal*, you know the wonders of collage creating, but refreshers are often useful. You're going to cull pleasing images from magazines and mail order catalogs, but the subject matter will be houses, furniture, homewares, decorating, gardening. When you see an image that you love, or one that elicits a visceral reaction of pleasure—we're searching for the "Wow!" factor—tear it out. You'll really be delighted and surprised with how powerful this process can be for moving beyond the slough of despair to contentment.

To get started, go to a newsstand and treat yourself to a few home shelter magazines, especially ones you don't normally read. Don't forget to peruse foreign publications for some of your images. Experiment with British women's magazines because they are so completely different in layout and design from our homegrown ones; their fresh visuals always get my creative juices going. Another magazine to source for beautiful images is the late, long-lamented, and sorely missed *Victoria*. (I've been lucky getting back copies on eBay.)

Spend the next month gathering your images and separate them into envelopes labeled Foyer and Hallways; Living Rooms; Kitchens; Dining Rooms; Family Rooms; Bedrooms; Bathrooms; Storage; Home Offices; Play Rooms; Sanctuaries; Personal Spa; Gardens and Outdoor Structures; Fabrics, Colors and Wallpaper; Lighting Fixtures; and I've Always Wanted.

Think fun. Think delight. Think seven years old and paper dolls. This is not an intellectual exercise. This is a meditative insight tool, as well as a playmate, to help you begin to think about your home in a fresh way.

"Can't nothing make your life work if you ain't the architect," Terry McMillan reminds us. Your House of Belonging must be built from the inside out by your heart, not your head.

NESTING INSTINCTS:
SEASONAL SERENITY

What to do with a half-used roll of Valentine's Day tissue paper, the resusable Easter decorations, or a dozen cups and napkins with jack-o-lanterns on them that are left over from your Halloween party? Why save them for next year, of course. But this year, store them so that you can find them again next year.

—Donna Smallin

All well and good the concept of storing the holiday decorations where we can find them; however, by the time New Year's rolls around and every needle has dropped, all a woman wants to do is ransom her home back from the holidays. So as we take down the tree, many of us toss everything into the first box available or the last one open and shove them away with abandon. This is how you end up warehousing more boxes of Christmas Past than at the North Pole. Like all mystery formulas, compound holiday clutter—using the sliding scale that each year the fewer decorations you actually put up, the more boxes you eventually store—guarantees misery before we next make merry.

Woman, get thee to a large emporium where they specialize in storage containers; even better if they're storage boxes designed specifically for Christmas decorations, wrapping paper, ribbons, etc. As you gather together your supplies, visualize the thrill and amazement of finding the stockings in the box labeled "Stockings," the lights in the box labeled "Tree Lights," or "Outdoor Lights" with all the lights wound in neat and tidy strings around a cardboard paper towel roll (this works!). How good does that feel? It doesn't take much to make us happy. Unfortunately, the sorry truth is, as Marcelene Cox wrote in 1947: "Happiness is not something you get, but something you do." Like putting things away the way we want to find them.

Now go through all the boxes you didn't open this year. What's in them? With our living arrangements changing so frequently—children grow up, move away, marriages end through death or divorce—Christmas ornaments often become poignant footnotes. After the holidays is the perfect time to sort them because the emotional expectations that surround the holidays have passed. Separate the guilt stashes from legitimate decorations you might want to pass on to your children when they have households of their own. You don't have to keep the crochet ornaments made by your former mother-in-law any longer, and a fossilized macaroni wreath loses its charm when its creator starts shaving. If you think any former family ornaments might be appreciated, pass them on with a smile. To help you decide what stays and goes, imagine your children going through the boxes after you've departed the scene. Do you hear them saying in exasperation, "What was She thinking, saving this?" or do you hear them sighing softly, "Oh, Mommy, you made the most beautiful Christmases for us...." Personally, I don't want a dry eye in the attic after I'm gone, which means I'd rather they sort memories than messes.

While you're sifting and sorting your decorations into neat boxes, label one of them, "Advent." When my daughter was little I used to keep the Advent wreath base in here, along with her wooden Advent calendar and other decorations I'd want on December 1. Now I store all our holiday music CDs, videos, DVDs, and favorite Christmas cookbooks in the Advent box. It's always a treat to open it up. Is it because I know what's in there? Probably.

The English travel writer and photographer Dame Freya Madeline Stark believed that "Christmas is not an external event at all, but a piece of one's home that one carries in one's heart." On any given day of the year, a woman's heart feels torn in a thousand directions at once. But the gift of organized seasonal storage will keep on giving next Christmas and beyond. And if Christmas is neat, tidy, and serenely tucked away, can New Year's Eve paper horns and Valentine's Day tissue paper be that far away?

HEART REFLECTIONS:
THE BELOVED OFFERS A PSALM FOR DOMESTIC BLISS

*D*earest Master Builder, we thank and praise you for the gifts of Simple Abundance and the blessings of domestic bliss. Mother of the Hearth and Father of Homecoming, hear our prayer. Generous Providers of Sacred Space, bless this woman, my dearly beloved Reader, and the home in which she lives and loves. Thank you for the haven of hospitality she has discovered in her home this day; we Bless you for the shelter that protects her Soul this night. Thank you that the solace of a home which embraces, nurtures, sustains, and comforts is part of Your Divine Blueprint for our happiness. Bless the foundation upon which she walks, the walls that surround, the roof that covers, the windows that allow light, and the threshold that welcomes her and hers. With the gift of each day may her love and gratefulness increase. May the peace and plenty she so richly shares with others always be her daily portion. Lead her, Divine Architect, with thanksgiving to the sanctuary you have set apart for her heart— her blessed, beloved House of Belonging.

Be it done, with all praise and honor according to Thee and accepted with thanksgiving by She.

CHAPTER TWO

CALLING ALL GIRLS

ON WOMEN AND DOMESTIC BLISS

I have no home but me.

—Anne Truitt

POSY AND THE HOPEFULS

September 1959: A young girl shuffles home from school alone, shoulders hunched, head down. She chokes back the tears, wiping them away with her yellow sweater sleeve, and when the street becomes a watery blur beneath her feet, she stops to catch her breath and pull up her knee socks.

Bewildered by the intensity of her emotions—shame, embarrassment, humiliation—she quickens her pace once her house comes into view. Running now, she soon hears her mother and little brother beyond the kitchen's screen door. To avoid uncomfortable questions, she sneaks in through the front and bolts up the stairs, closing her bedroom door behind her.

Their voices came quite clearly to Posy's ears as she passed the assembly hall doors.

*"Oh **no**, not Posy Tennant. She'd **never** fit in with the Group. Can you imagine tubby, messy Posy being chosen Queen of the Harvest Festival?"*

It was Lana Paul's voice—clear, amused, and scornful.

"I guess you're right, Lana," Dody Moore hesitated, then, "Posy wouldn't fit in in a group of hopeful queens."

"But definitely not!"

"You can say that again!"

The voices came fast now, tumbling over each other... "After all, if we're to be known as The Hopefuls, we've got to live up to the qualifications. The prettiest, the neatest, the smartest girl is always chosen for Browning Junior High's festival queen!"

*"And Posy Tennant just isn't any of **those** things, if you know what I mean!"*

*"I know what you mean. Did you see her skirt today? It was **safety-pinned together**. And her hair—my dear!"*

"Her hair is always a fright. She..."

But Posy didn't want to hear any more...so she stopped her ears, but she couldn't stop her mind.

Neither could I after I read the story "Posy and the Hopefuls" (by Elizabeth Rainbow) in my favorite preteen magazine, *Calling All Girls.* "Days merge into days," Rosamunde Pilcher tells us, "so that dissociated vignettes, beyond chronology, stay in the mind." In creating my own House of Belonging, I've discovered it's often the dissociated vignettes that yield the most subtle and profound insights which heal secret wounds. With stunning clarity, once again I'm walking down Lowell Street, crying, hurrying home to hide in my bedroom. I'm not Posy, but she *is* me.

Then she looked around her room.

The bed was still unmade. The jeans and shirt she'd worn yesterday were flung over a chair. Magazines littered the floor. Her dresser top was a clutter of bobby pins, crumpled tissues, records, books, and papers.

The bundle of soiled clothes she'd meant to take down to the laundry this morning was on her desk along with a half dozen empty pop bottles....

Posy saw a half-eaten candy bar on the table beside her bed. She walked eagerly toward it, then stopped.

Tubby. Fatty... She looked at her reflection in the wall mirror. She saw the safety-pin Taffy Lynn had snickered over. The button had snapped from her waistband this morning, and it had been easier to pin it together instead of hunting for a needle and thread. Besides, the skirt was too tight anyway. An untidy gap showed her white slip. Her sweater was too tight also. It hiked up at the back, and the buttoned front strained apart in little gaps like her skirt....

How astonishing it is to discover yourself on the page for the first time! To excavate your inner girl. I was 10 and the intimacy of seeing myself through Posy's eyes was as eerie as it was reassuring. I didn't need to hide any longer; there was another girl who knew how I felt, who shared my pain, and who wouldn't betray my shame.

She looked once more at the ugly gap in her skirt, her stretched sweater, her fat—yes fat—face, and tangled, unbrushed curls.

"Face it, Rose Louise Tennant," she said slowly. "You're exactly what they called you—a messy, fatty, tubby, blot on the horizon!"

Her eyes suddenly spilled over. She wanted to throw herself on the bed and cry and cry, but something held her back—a little flame that had all at once sparked within her—a flame of angry pride.

"I'll show them," she said to the disordered room. "I'll show them whether or not I'm fit to join their old Hopeful Group!"

She picked up the candy she had dropped, and threw it in the trash basket. She hung her jeans and shirt in the closet. She made the bed. She looked despairingly at the dresser, then with a determined shrug sailed into the mess. An hour later the room was tidy, and Posy went down to dinner.

Posy was my first literary dose of self-help. I read her story compulsively, especially the parts where she begins to clean her room: You mean pretty, smart, neat, well-groomed girls weren't born that way? They were made? If Posy could change her life, I could too. I walked into a revival tent on the pages of *Calling All Girls* and was baptized in the Church of Improbable Happy Endings. My abiding faith sustains me to this day. When I began my research for this book, I knew I wanted to discover where the stitch had been dropped in the fabric of my domesticity. As I thought about my homemaking memories, Posy's story gleamed like a golden thread in a flax sampler; to find it, I scoured the Internet for as many past issues of *Calling All Girls* as I could find. Anyone old enough to remember this monthly, palm-size magazine with its redemptive pulp fiction and cheery how-tos knows what I mean. Although *Calling All Girls'* cute blond cover girl probably bore little resemblance to its readers, I adored her easy good looks, great outfits, seasonal costumes, and adorable dachshund.

In recalling the simple, magnetic pull of Posy, I believe it was the first time I had an everyday epiphany. I suddenly realized that people could alter their circumstances and change their lives, not overnight, not by magic, but with persistence and moxie: one tiny choice, day by day. What's more, as Posy's story so engagingly revealed, I began to see a cosmic connection between personal grooming and domestic bliss.

You see, after Posy picked up her room, her mood shifted from despair to optimism; the sight of her neat room gave her a sense of serenity and pride. In fact, she felt so encouraged that she immediately changed her eating habits by passing on the gravy and her favorite coconut cream pie. After dinner she took a bath, not as a slapdash chore but as a "beauty ritual," which, again, was a tremendous shift in attitude; she scrubbed her nails, shampooed her hair, and walked around her room with a book on her head before doing her homework. The next morning she rose early to dress in a leisurely way and to fix her hair nicely. For exercise she volunteered to help her dad with the gardening, and when she was thirsty, drank iced tea and water instead of soda pop. Posy's pluck was so persuasive, I began to make similar changes. I wanted to be just like her.

A month later, my first heroine could button all her skirts, got straight A's on her report card, and kept her room so tidy that her mother redecorated it in pink and white. Everyone was impressed with the new, improved Posy, including The Hopefuls.

Lana gazed admiringly at the trim rose wool dress that Mom had made for Posy. . . .

"How pretty you look, Posy," she said, "and I guess you're mighty proud of having your composition judged the best in history class!"

Then she added confidentially, "Look, gal—Meta, Taffy, Scrap, and Dody are coming over to my house tonight. We're all hoping to be the one selected queen, and we're sort of grooming ourselves for the big moment. We call ourselves The Hopefuls. Would you like to join us, Posy?"

Her smile was warm and friendly. But Posy averted her eyes from it and hardened her heart.

"Thanks, but no thanks," she said coldly.

She had finished her salad and butterless roll, and she got up from the table and walked out of the lunch room.

"I'm beginning to show them at last!" she told herself triumphantly. But somehow the triumph didn't feel as glorious as she had thought it would. She felt herself wanting to turn back to Lana's warm smile.

Actually, I didn't remember this part of the story. What I do remember was Hooray, Queen Posy! She went from being a tubby, messy girl, like me, to the most popular girl in school. Posy represented the triumph of true grit and amazing grace: a poster girl for self-determination. And that's where her story ended—I thought.

NO MOTHER TO GUIDE HER

Homesickness seems to me one of the most terrible maladies, and one which you do not necessarily outgrow with age. It lies in wait like a recurrent illness, and sometimes, quite unexpectedly, the old familiar pain will surge over you.

—Ilka Chase

Through the years I've wondered what became of Posy. Did she turn out to be a good homemaker, or did she end up like me? Posy may have turned her life around in a month, but by the time she became Harvest Queen, I'd already resumed my slipshod ways, longing to grow up to be a domestic Girl Guide but remaining one of sloth's handmaidens to this day. Now I realize in a way that I couldn't when I was young that one of the keys to Posy's success was her mother's encouragement—preparing meals that helped her stick to her diet, altering her clothes as she lost weight, and making her new dresses to show off her emerging figure. As Posy kept her room neat, mother and daughter looked through magazines together, plotting and planning how the two of them would redo her bedroom. They were a terrific team. They were also so real to me in that way fictional characters can be when you're in your wonder years; secretly I believed that this was how every mother and daughter interacted—if the daughter was just "good" enough, so that her mother would be proud of her.

What kind of a homemaking relationship did you have with your mother? Did she patiently show you how to fold clothes, iron a blouse, make a bed, or knead bread? Did she demonstrate how to polish a table, put up preserves, prune a rose bush, hang a curtain, or hem a skirt? Some women grew up with mothers who taught them the art of homemaking; not just sharing family recipes and household hints but instructing them how to cream the butter, fold fitted sheets, thread a needle; passing on a priceless domestic dowry. Mothers "performing the rituals of the ordinary as an act of faith," Marilynne Robinson tells us in her exquisite novel *Housekeeping,* knowing that the "dear ordinary heals" and imparting this sacred truth to their daughters.

My friend Peg was one such lucky girl, and I often thought that if I couldn't be Posy, I would have loved being Peggy. I'll never forget the first time I saw her room: it was spotless! And so pretty! Polished maple furniture, white chenille bedspread, pink rosebud ruffled curtains, fringed throw rugs. "Does your mother clean your room?" I whispered incredulously, for surely no human girl was capable of this level of domestic accomplishment. "No," she told me with a proud smile. *She did!* But her mom had taught her how to do everything.

Another time, in junior high, I visited a friend's home, and Jill was ironing her blouses for the week, using spray starch and carefully pressing not only the front and collar but the *back* of her blouse *even though it would be covered by a sweater*. We were 13! These enviable girls became true domestic goddesses as far as I was concerned and several decades later were the women who couldn't understand what the fuss was about when Martha Stewart assumed the role of America's Mommie Dearest.

As one dearly cherished wag put it, "I just don't get it. What kid *didn't* have her mother show her how to sew on a button?" Well, my kid, for one. Heaven knows I probably have a lot of other stuff to answer for, but letting my daughter grow up believing missing buttons are repaired at the dry cleaners makes me wince. I should have picked up the gypsy's warnings when Katie was 4 and her favorite video wasn't *My Little Pony* but Martha making canapés. Then I just thought it was so cute, the way she'd sit mesmerized by the flower-shaped crudités; for weeks she wanted to prepare heart-shape melba toast to take as her nursery snack. Of course, I did it for her, entirely missing the opportunity being presented to both of us. What was I thinking? Really, Mother, she wanted to do it herself. Most of the women I know would rather be caught having sex with a complete stranger in a phone booth than confess to two acts of maternal turpitude: taking a nap and revealing what their children don't know about housekeeping. Lately there is an epidemic of "crowded nest" syndrome—adult children returning to live with their parents instead of fleeing the coop. Who can blame them? I suspect it has little to do with economics and much to do with the fact that we never taught them how to create a home for themselves. In our defense, may I offer the Anita Loos' excuse: no mother to guide *us*.

For women whose homemaking mentors were Donna Reed and June Cleaver, excavating your domestic history can seem daunting, but it's a necessary part of coping with the emotional turmoil that engulfs you every day, thwarting your ability to achieve contentment. "Coming to understand our mothers and why they behave as they do—or as they did—around the house is partly just a function of getting older," Margaret Horsfield reassures us in *Biting the Dust: The Joys of Housework*. But "to have more sympathy for our mothers, to come to see their household patterns more clearly, is one step towards understanding how [our] domestic history has unfolded and how it continues to unfold in our own lives."

Sometimes when we travel back, unwelcome memories arrive unexpectedly, like a third cousin and her family who drop in because they're "just passing through." We remember the girl who always felt like an outsider, who served punch at the dance rather than taking to the floor herself, who quickly passed the popular kids' hangout so that no one would suspect how much she wanted to be invited to join them. You may remember finding the contents of your dresser dumped on the bedroom floor and being locked in your room until it was clean, instead of going out with your friends. Maybe we remember a young girl who had too many adult responsibilities, like cooking supper for her sisters and brothers while Mom rested on the sofa every afternoon. Today she's a celebrated chef, which just shows you how far a girl can go with a can opener and Dinty Moore beef stew. And when journalists ask if her mother was a big influence on her career, she smiles and says, "Absolutely, she was my inspiration. I couldn't have done it without her."

Through death, illness, addiction, abuse, or neglect, the spilt milk of forsaken childhood touches us all. There might be a perfectly plausible explanation for how you learned that a house is not necessarily a home, or why I didn't. Nonetheless this flawed building block can become the Divine foundation for creating your House of Belonging. *All our past asks of us is to remember.* When each of us acknowledges our little Posy with compassion, respect, and reverence, we ransom back the girls we left behind, discovering, as writer Esther Hautzig reminds us, "a young girl's heart is indestructible."

OUR MOTHERS OURSELVES

The holes we leave for our daughters are for them to darn with the yarn of their own lives. Just as we did. Just as we are doing.
—Isabelle Huggan

I don't remember my mother as a slattern who never got out of her nightgown before noon; I remember an attractive woman in neatly ironed shirtwaists, pearls, heels, pretty ruffled aprons, perfectly coiffed hair. Her name was Dru Donnelly and by the time I'd left home in the late '60s to find my fame and fortune, she'd turned three houses into warm, cozy, inviting homes for her family. Mother was a consummate decorator, wonderful cook, and marvelous hostess. She excelled at handicrafts from sewing to woodworking. Her Halloween costumes were legendary, and living up to the birthday parties she orchestrated for her four children daunts me even now. I remember Mom knocking down walls and discovering hidden fireplaces, refinishing flea market finds, and making slipcovers. But I also remember that by the age of 10 I was slovenly, overweight, and didn't realize that the back of my hair needed to be combed until someone at school asked if I was building a nest back there.

Unfortunately, I didn't get the kind of nest-building advice I needed, and perhaps you didn't either—on how to keep house.

"Many middle-aged women of today had mothers who were dissatisfied housewives. These mothers taught their daughters not to get trapped but to get their degree and go out into the world and fulfill the mothers' frustrated ambitions. In droves, the daughters did just this—overall, a good thing," Cheryl Mendelson explains in *Home Comforts: The Art and Science of Keeping House.*

However, the dire consequences of sending their daughters out into the world minus aprons, never mind bras, resulted in a generation of women who often broke the glass ceiling but still don't know the proper way to load a dishwasher. She adds, "Many young women have confided to me sadly that they felt sometimes as though they were being driven from things feminine and domestic by mothers who would not let them help cook or teach them anything of the mothers' own domestic crafts, no matter how much the daughters wanted to learn them."

But that was then, and this is now. And while there is some truth that we can't ever go home again, what we can do is cherish, celebrate, and consecrate our own homecoming, one replaced button at a time. We begin by acknowledging the role that homemaking is *meant* to play in our lives. It doesn't matter what your mother may have wanted for you. It matters what you want for yourself. It seems almost impossible to believe, but in the last 50 years of "progress," nearly a millennia of domestic knowledge has fallen through the cracks of social history. Reclaiming lost homekeeping arts is how we ground ourselves back into the Real, even if we work 9 a.m. to 5 p.m., Monday through Friday. A clean kitchen and an executive corner office are not mutually exclusive; in fact, I know I work better all day if I take care of just two tasks before I leave the house in the morning—make the bed and empty the kitchen sink.

A "sense of being at home is important to everyone's well-being. If you do not get enough of it, your happiness, resilience, energy, humor, and courage will decrease," Cheryl Mendelson explains. "Being at home feels safe; you have a sense of relief whenever you come home and close the door behind you...." Coming home each day is meant to be "your major restorative in life."

The homemaker of yesterday knew that it took more than just dusting and vacuuming to make a home feel warm and alive. "Her real secret was that she identified herself with her home," Cheryl Mendelson confides. Her self-respect was reflected "in the soft sofa cushions, clean linens, and good meals; her memory in well-stocked storeroom cabinets and the pantry; her intelligence in the order and healthfulness of her home; her good humor in its light and air. She lived her life not only through her body but through the house as an extension of her body."

BLEAK HOUSE

> *If you want the honest spiritual truth, my prayer is this: Dear God, get me out of this mess.*
>
> —Rita Mae Brown

I don't know which is worse, remembering a painful past or ignoring an excruciating present. But I do know what they have in common: clutter. I also know that moving on isn't as much about taking a few steps forward as it is about being willing to untangle and then ruthlessly uproot whatever's holding us back.

As I look around my study at the stacks of books on the floor waiting to be reshelved; piles of files, mail, and magazines; sweaters; scarves; slippers; teacups; odd socks; lip gloss; eyeglasses; empty prescription bottles (memo to self, call for refills), it's difficult to believe that this is the working space of the writer of *Simple Abundance,* which established Order as a life-changing principle. Gone are the office overlooking Rockefeller Plaza and the luxury of personal assistants. (I know you won't believe this, but at one point I had nine of them in two countries. God knows I *wish* I were making this up. But at least one of them knew how to keep files and rein in disorder.) The kitchen counters are crowded with the detritus of my new life as a wife once again, and as a stepmother for the first time (two fabulous teenage boys— both as handsome, funny, intelligent, and charming as their English father). Blessed am I among women, and I know it.

However, my closets are so crammed that the doors won't shut completely, and I'm hard pressed to distinguish whether it's too many clothes or an identity crisis bulging at the seams. My drawers don't just hide disorder; they hoard it. I don't want to find the tube of cold sore cream behind the cereal boxes; I want it returned to the medicine chest *where it belongs.* I don't want to run upstairs and rummage in the den for the corkscrew or ransom a clean towel from the dryer. The chaos that engulfs me is so disheartening, it stops me dead in my tracks. I pick something up to put away only to look around in appalled fascination and set it back down somewhere else. While a passionate homemaker dwells in my heart, it's the messy girl who occupies my house. No wonder I don't feel as if I belong here; I don't.

Are these your secret musings too? How did we get into this mess? What's really preventing us from enjoying sustainable serenity in our surroundings? For instance, if we know to hang it up when we take it off, why do we toss it on the bedroom chair? On days when I can't figure out *what* to wear in the morning, I return in the evening to a bedroom resembling a place where volunteers sort piles of donated clothing for the victims of natural disasters. It's enough to make a grown woman cry—and often it does. If you also find yourself hovering on the verge of hysterics, there are many triggers: you could be coming down with something, it could be raging hormones, the fight you had with your husband this morning, your job's unreasonable demands, or your teenager's pierced tongue; it could also be the end of a long day in which you couldn't call 15 minutes your own because it would take 20 to clear a comfortable place to sit down.

Small miseries eventually pile up and extract a usurious price. Benign neglect becomes self-abuse. Despite all our good intentions and every book we've bought (but not read) on organizing, we end up spiritual spendthrifts squandering something more precious than money: our time, creative energy, and emotions. Our self-respect. Our future. Our dreams. So much of our day is spent in retracing our steps, reliving yesterday or last week looking for what we've lost or misplaced, that we're blind to the Simple Abundance that literally surrounds and stuns us. How can we expect (or even ask) the Universe to gift us with more good in our life if we've not got space for it?

For it's not only the desk, bedroom, or house that's untidy. Messy habits leak into other areas of our lives. We let nasty comments go unanswered or a relationship that could use attention sit unattended. It might be that we think we're avoiding confrontation as long as we can still go about our business, undetected or unchallenged. But, then, as Anaïs Nin confesses, the moment comes when we "cannot bear outer pressures anymore," and so the only remedy is to declare war on ourselves and wage hand-to-hand combat with our belongings: "As if unable to organize and control my life, I seek to exert this on a world of objects." With a ferocious but futile fervor we dig ourselves out one day, only to bury ourselves alive at the weekend. What does it profit a woman to gain the kitchen junk drawer only to lose the hall closet? A house divided will never be serene. A life divided will always come undone.

DO TRY THIS AT HOME:
PERSONAL EFFECTS

Live in the layers
Not on the litter.

—Stanley Kunitz

Most organizational experts approach clutter as the enemy that needs to be conquered. Not just defeated, but crushed. Vanquished. However, I've learned that clutter often comes into our lives as an ally, an unexpected friend arriving when our subconscious believes we need rescuing.

Think of clutter as co-dependent; we allow clutter to accumulate and it enables us to continue to stay stagnant in an unhealthy situation that should have been dealt with years ago. In fact, we've been discontented for so long, we begin to think of discomfort as "normal." We refuse to acknowledge that this painful condition exists, rather like rubbing a blister on the heel of your foot until it becomes calloused. Although our souls long to move on, our weary hearts are so sad and scared by the loss implied in letting go that our mind calls in psychological reinforcements— entropy's Special Forces.

Imagine a military SWAT team arriving at your door. But instead of blackened faces, fatigues, and guns aloft, they're dressed in soccer Mom khakis with grass-stained knees, unpaid bills sticking out of their helmets, and brandishing broken umbrellas. Watch as they blend into each room to bolster inertia's insidious takeover of your life. Clutter cleverly adopts the color, shape, texture, and tension of your surroundings and then settles in for the long haul, which isn't likely to be to the Dumpster.

During the writing of *Simple Abundance*, I confronted my messy girl, or at the very least, had meaningful conversations with her. I was honest, loving, and resolute; believing that a hard-core co-dependent will change behavior without intervention is wishful thinking. Still, clutter and I came to a working arrangement, as long as I stuck to my housekeeping routine. On the surface, everything seemed contained. Then *Simple Abundance* got popular and the state of my house disintegrated as dramatically as the fall of the Roman Empire. Circumstances beyond my control, you might think, as did I. I was busier than ever. I didn't have time for housekeeping. I figured that an orderly household of three people should be able to maintain itself, especially if you've established rituals, which I had.

Still, no matter how many drawers, closets, and shelves I rearranged on the weekend, clutter and confusion came back at an alarming rate. No sooner had I put away a stack of clean towels found loitering on the dining room table than I would find more waiting to be washed downstairs. It was if the towels were using themselves. Kitchen drawers started rearranging their contents; things I kept on my nightstand appeared on my dresser; an odd assortment of books from my office ended up on the coffee table; CDs from the living room ended up in the bedroom. I began to feel incredibly uneasy.

"It's the weirdest thing," I said to a deeply spiritual friend. "It's as if I suddenly have poltergeists coming in to undo whatever progress I make."

"Sounds like you need an exorcism," she joked, but not really. Then she recommended that I consult a "house buster," an English psychic who performed energy readings on houses to see if there were any metaphysical blockages. Her expertise was finding not those things preventing you from selling your house, but the ones that stop you from living happily in it.

"She'll just tell me I'm having a hard time dealing with success," I laughed. "Oh, all right. But for Heaven's sake, *don't* tell her who I am; use my married name. I'd be mortified if this mess ever went public."

CLUTTER-DEPENDENT NO MORE

> *There are no new truths, but only truths that have not been recognized by those who have perceived them without noticing.*
>
> —Mary McCarthy

I was mystified when the psychic asked if the house had a history of violence; the readings she picked up were very sad. She told me that the house was "weeping." It was traumatized like a woman after a physical assault. The psychic told me that the energy of the house had shut down and was not cooperating with me because it was grievously wounded. The disorder and tumult were an outward manifestation of betrayal. "A woman's sacred space has been violated. The spirit of the house is protecting her in the only way it knows how, beneath the clutter and confusion. The house is trying to hide her from the intruders. The real disarray is deceit."

Shocked by this analysis, my friend and I challenged the psychic's findings. I was aghast at her implication. The psychic shrugged and said that she was only reporting the aura readings she was picking up. Did I want a healing ritual performed for the house or not?

"Okay," I said. "Because you're here…Might as well."

The woman said she would treat for the Truth to be revealed. "It's the clutter I want to get rid of," I told her. She said, "Uncover the truth and the clutter will vanish." A month later, my marriage came to an abrupt end when I discovered the secret my house had known for years. It never occurred to my husband, he told me in tears, that when he invited his longtime *friend* to our home in my absence, he was "violating" my sacred space. He was just being practical. He wanted to be there to answer the phone if I called. I was the woman clutter was trying to protect, just as I was using clutter to hide from betrayal. The house buster was right; my clutter disappeared.

Clutter is "not just about clearing a physical space. It's an emotional and spiritual act," says the English writer Lesley Garner. "Like all acts of emotional and spiritual significance, the act of clearing out can be surrounded by deep resistance. I only have to lay hands on a well-loved old jacket or a jar of assorted screws for my mind to start screaming, 'You can't get rid of that!' Things of sentimental value are the worst. They develop psychic tendrils and draw me in. Old letters and photographs stick to my fingers and refuse to be thrown away. Instead they bind me to them, insisting that I hear their story once again. 'We're family history,' they rustle insidiously. 'You can't get rid of us.... [but] once you pay attention to your possessions in this way you realize they have a life of their own. And sometimes the day comes when their life with you is over and you both need to move on. The word that has the power here is 'move.' Movement is life."

Clutter is much more than objects that lie on the surface of our lives. Begin thinking of clutter as the tip of what lies beneath, struggling to show its face. Clutter "symbolizes what is outworn and unfulfilled in our lives," Lesley Garner notes. "That is why it is so very hard to give away and clear out because that is an acknowledgement of hard truth. It means admitting that I will never be a size 10 again, he will never love me again, I will never read *War and Peace* and the children won't be coming back home. I admit it. What is left after that is reality and truth and space. That is a wonderful place to let go of the past and begin the rest of your life."

SARAH BAN BREATHNACH

SHOW AND TELL

Most new discoveries are suddenly-seen things that were always there.

—Susanne K. Langer

So what's clutter done for you lately? Not much you say. In fact, it's driving you mad. So how about approaching clutter in a new way: as a friend offering help. Remember the candid camera shots you were going to take of the different rooms and clutter hot spots in your house? We need them now because you're going to paste each photograph on a separate page in your *House of Belonging Companion*. After you've done that, put the book away for a day or so to recover from the shock of the pictures.

Next, carve out a 20-minute interlude for a little detective meditative musing; you're going to become your own clutter coach. Put on some soothing music, pour a glass of good cheer, and, pen in hand, look at one of the photos and ask yourself questions, such as:

- What's clutter trying to tell you?

- What does this woman worry about?

- Who shares her house?

- How long has that bulb needed replacing?

- Why doesn't she finish crafts projects?

Don't discount anything that comes into your head. Clutter knows if you're an eBay addict or have a shoe fetish. It also knows why a lot of your mail doesn't get opened. Try this exercise on a Sunday or Monday night; then during the week just glance at the pictures for five minutes before you go to sleep. That's it. Look but don't touch! Do not, if you can help it, start to dismantle the hot spot before the end of the week. Why? Because by *not* allowing yourself to clear away the clutter, but only thinking about why it's there in the first place, you'll be desperate to devote the one hour necessary to clearing it. You'll be amazed and thrilled at how fast you plow through it. That's because your subconscious mind has been sifting and sorting all week long.

Let's say the hot spot you're focusing on is a bedroom chair buried beneath weeks of discards—fat pants, tight tops, a skirt with a torn zipper, the soiled, the spoiled, the impulse buys still in the bags. Normally, you'd reach a point where the stuff would get shuffled but not necessarily dispatched. Not so quick, babe. Not this time. By encouraging yourself to just look and think about one hot spot at a time, you make Clutter Busting something to be desired, not dreaded. You'll be surprised at how, week by week, you begin to reclaim your space.

But *beware*. You'll feel so proud of yourself as you blitz through your target area, more energetic and optimistic than you ever believed possible, that you may be inspired to do more at one time. Don't be! That so-called "voice" egging you on is Clutter's siren song. She knows if she lures you into too much at once, you'll never finish and end up on the rocky shoals of good intentions.

So when you're done with each hot spot, stop. And give thanks for unsung friends in unexpected places. Remember Posy? Well, what I didn't recall after all these years was the end of her story. After Posy is chosen Queen of the Harvest Festival, guess what happens? She discovers the first *Simple Abundance* principle—Gratitude.

Posy, her head whirling with success and triumph, saw the five Hopefuls hovering uncertainly on the edge of the crowd and thought:

This is the big payoff. This is where I pay them back for calling me tubby and messy. They won't even figure in the Festival. I can pick my own handmaidens, and it won't be them—you can bet!

And then, suddenly, Posy's breath caught in her throat, as a new thought burst like a rocket in her brain.... Why shouldn't she thank the Hopefuls? They were just as responsible for start-ing her on her way towards becoming a queen.... It was because of The Hopefuls that she had learned to eat right and lose her fat; learned to keep herself trim and attractive. They were respon-sible for her excellent grades, her lovely new pink-and-white bedroom at home!

"Why, they've been my friends all the time!" Posy told herself wonderingly, "even if they weren't aware of it. They were my friends by being critical, by noticing that I wasn't pretty, or neat, or smart. They made me queen just as much as I made myself!" Her friends...

"Thanks, pals," she whispered gratefully, "thanks a million!"

NESTING INSTINCTS:
THE SCENTED LINEN CLOSET

It is everything I long for....
—Audrey Hepburn

A cupboard, a cupboard, any kingdom for a cupboard. In fact, if all the world were mine—from the sea to the Rhine—I would happily give it all up for just one large, walk-in, proper linen closet.

Close your eyes for a moment and let an azure-lidded fantasy flood your mind's eye. You open a white door. There, on lace-edged, deep wooden shelves, you find row after row of neat and tidy willow baskets piled high with perfectly folded sheets; fleecy blankets; fluffy terry cloth; crisp starched, white damask table-cloths; pristine napkins; monogrammed linen tea towels; pillow slips with the patina of the past edged in cotton crochet. Around the bountiful bundles are pale French silk ribbons tied in perfect bows. You stand transfixed before this eighth wonder of the world, a treasure worthy of John Keats' traders' tales from "silken Samarcand to cedar'd Lebanon." The air is perfumed with an intoxicating fragrance. A sigh of exquisite pleasure escapes your lips. It will be yours. It will.

Well, it might be yours, but a decade after I conjured up this feminine reverie in *Simple Abundance*, it still isn't mine. (Frankly, I doubt you've gotten any further than I have.)

Not for the lack of trying or tying, mind you. We can tie French silk ribbons with the best of them, and our collection of vintage pillowcases is prodigious. Still, if what you see when you open up your linen closet is a jumble sale, perhaps it's time for us to move on to a more achievable fantasy, *chérie*.

Then again, maybe not. As the late, great Mary Cantwell lamented, when women order their linens into ranks it is a form of self-defense in a disorderly world. "There was not, is not, a thing to be done about pestilence, death and the bad dreams that sneak up on us when we're not sleeping. But I would have had that cupboard, that proof positive that I could make tidy my minuscule corner of the universe." I think she's on to something here. The key word is "minuscule," as in small masterpiece; something attainable. A drawer, perhaps, before a closet. But first may I point out that a proper linen cupboard is not a frivolous indulgence? It's an essential. Soul nurturing, sanity preserving, homeopathic medicine. We know the difference between a passing whim and a true need. For what is the harried feminine heart seeking in stacks of the scented, orderly, and pristine? A vision that refreshes and restores. A solitary sensory delight of sight, fragrance, and hearing (that would be your contented sighs) which soothes as it energizes. And while that can happen occasionally with a cup of tea under an apple tree or in the hushed silence of early morning at the vacation cabin in Maine, this state of grace should also happen more often at home, at will. And it can, if we create small domestic nests to act as oases throughout a parched daily round. Think an aromatic, well-stocked pantry; a cheery, inspiring cubby devoted to baking supplies; an inviting vanity for our makeup; a cozy book nook; or a scented linen stash.

How to begin: Married or single, with or without children, it's pointless to pretend that we can keep the everyday sheets, towels, tablecloths, and napkins in the same storage area as the delicates, damask, and vintage tea towels that make our hearts beat faster. So the key to sustainable serenity is having not one big linen closet but four smaller storage spaces for bed, bath, table, and reverie.

During the Middle Ages, the mistress of the house stored her best linen in the bottom drawer of her wardrobe or armoire. She didn't need more room because she didn't have many "good" pieces of linen and they certainly weren't used for every day. But her drawer was scented with lavender, cloves, orange, and rose (originally to ward off pests), and her slender stacks were beribboned to keep them neat and tidy. During the 16th century, a separate chest became a popular wedding gift for brides. Containing her household "dowry," it had been lovingly prepared years in advance by the women members of the bride's family.

Reviving the romantic ritual of the scented linen drawer or chest is the perfect solution to our dilemma. Building a household linen dowry of your own is one of the most delightful treats you can imagine. After my sudden divorce I felt so adrift and bereft starting a new household from scratch. (I once burst into tears and abandoned the grocery cart when I couldn't find a garlic press as good as the one I'd left behind.) So on the weekends I'd go antiquing for "dowry" linens I'd never had as a bride. Start small. A drawer for now. It's never too late to begin self-nurturing through nesting.

HEART REFLECTIONS: THE BELOVED INVOKES HEAVEN UPON HER HEARTH

Mother of Plenty, Shield Against Want, hear the prayer of your Beloved, who asks with a grateful heart that she might receive her daily portion of Heaven today, upon her hearth. Provide me with the blessings of the House of Belonging: Light, Space, Warmth, and Solace. Thank you for those I love and those who love me. Thank you for the blessings of my health, which is my truest wealth. Thank you for my beautiful home and the discovery of five new blessings beneath its roof this day. Help me simplify some part of my life by endowing me with the time, creative energy, courage, and enthusiasm to bring order to one small surface of it: a drawer, a dresser, my desk. As I sift, sort, let go, and move past feelings of lack and distress, help me distinguish between my needs and my wants. Restore in me serenity and common sense as I pay my bills and balance my household accounts.

Remind me that my Source of Divine Replenishment, my Simple Abundance, is not to be found beyond the reach of my Soul and the desires of my heart. Thank you for the authentic gifts you have bestowed upon me alone, to make brighter the world and my place in it. If I am not fulfilling this birthright, if I have shied away because of failure, fear, or fatigue, give me the strength to honor my sacred bounty. Reveal to me one task that I might do today to increase both my faith and my fortune.

Wealth of the World, Provider of Peace, grant your dearly Beloved her blessing. Help me pull down the delights of Heaven upon my Hearth this day.

Be it done, with all praise and honor according to Thee and accepted with thanksgiving by She.

CHAPTER THREE

COME CELEBRATE HER HOME

ON WOMEN AND CHANGE

In my end is my beginning. That's a quotation I've often heard people say ... but what does it mean?

—Agatha Christie

ndings. Every beginning has one, damn it. And in between the endgame we never expected and the fresh start we never wanted lies a terrifying gap of uncertainty: the *Transition*. While we've begrudgingly become accustomed to the notion that "change" is the only constant in our lives, like Monty Python's Spanish Inquisition gag, no one *ever* expects the Transition that trawls in the wake of change. *No! No! Anything but the transition!*

But despite all the whinging, binging, flare-ups, wringing of hands, hangovers, bartering, and midnight eBay "finds" bought to distract us momentarily from the harrowing loss or amazing luck in bulldozing all that was familiar (both good and bad fortune trigger panic attacks), life's transitional phases do eventually shift shape as we become accustomed to our new situations. Still, like the last guest at the party, transitions don't disappear until we're good and ready for them to make an exit. Finally, we're willing to bid our farewells. Let go. Pass through. Get the hell out of our own way. Acknowledge, accept, appreciate. Well, maybe not go that far, yet. Still, at least take one step forward, which has been a long time in coming. We're ready to exhale, get our groove back. Move on.

Unfortunately, it's been my excruciating experience that all this gracious hospitality demands conscious and conspicuous consumption, the siphoning of a woman's most precious natural resources—time, creative energy, and emotion—which even on our best days is in dire supply.

The 13th-century mystic Rumi beautifully describes change and transition this way:

This being human is a guest house.
Every morning a new arrival.
A joy, a depression, a meanness,
Some momentary awareness comes
As an unexpected visitor.
Welcome and entertain them all!

Even if they're a crowd of sorrows,
Who violently sweep your house
Empty of its furniture,
Still, treat each guest honorably.
He may be clearing you out
For some new delight.

DAY TRIPPER

My days ran away so fast. I simply ran after my days.
—Leah Morton

When I started this chapter, I wondered if I wasn't avoiding the front door of our house for the same reason that I'd been avoiding emotional transitions all my life. Using the front door takes too much time to get where I need to be (usually the kitchen); it's awkward and narrow, which keeps me from hurtling through like a tornado.

Yes, woman, that's the point. But it's my choice every day —and yours as well. What door do you use?

Interesting and ironic diagnosis dilemma: Two weeks ago I was forced to go to the doctor because of debilitating episodes of dizziness and headaches. Having sustained two head injuries 20 years apart, I'm used to my head being my most sensitive threshold of pain, but these spinners were so severe I could barely lift it off the pillow. There was also the low droning of a buzz saw in between my ears. Definitely not the music of the spheres.

Sound familiar? Well, if like me you frequently don't know whether you're coming, going, or where you've been; if you often feel as if you're whirling so fast it's sheer centrifugal force that keeps you upright, then, sweetie, you're reeling for a very good reason. No, you are not the time traveler's wife. And I'm not Kim Novak in *Vertigo*.

"Please don't tell me it's stress," I said to my physician in the nicest possible way, trying to cut him off at the pass. "I know I'm stressed."

"Do you also know that yours is the behavior of a highly fraught, anxious, extremely neurotic woman?" asked the doctor, not so nicely.

"That's a bit harsh."

He means my new sleepwalking habit; it seems I'm rearranging pictures on the wall in the middle of the night. It's freaking the husband. (I don't think that's *so* weird. When do I get the chance during the day?) I began the litany of all the reasons I couldn't make life changes right at this moment. Soon, I reassured him, when I'm not so busy, there would be some changes made.

"Well, I can give you a million reasons why you must start some of those changes *today*. The dizziness is *vestibular dysfunction*. Motion sickness, the kind you experience riding in the backseat of a car, except you're stationary. Do you see how much you fidget? You're having trouble sitting still; you're extremely restless. Do you have a pressing need to be somewhere else right now?"

A pressing need? To be somewhere else? Now there's a question no woman doctor would ever ask. Because what woman, including the doctor, doesn't have a pressing need to be a million places at once?

I told him I had a deadline and needed to be back at my desk as soon as possible. After I discovered I wasn't dying at that moment (thank you, God), I asked what caused vestibular dysfunction and what I could do to stop it. Now.

"Quit multitasking. Work regular hours, and less, not more of them. Take two ten-minute walks every day, before sitting down at your desk and immediately after leaving it. Eat three meals a day and two small snacks. Drink more water than you do wine. Go to bed at the same time every night, no later than 9 p.m. And give your husband the hammer until you've finished the book. By the way, what are you writing about?"

"Women and *vestibules*."

Foyers. Vestibules. Entryways. Transition points, the lot of them.

On your way in, the first vibrations of a home; on your way out, the last safe space before emerging into the world. Looking at how I've dealt with change in my life, it's no wonder I'm in a spin as I write about the space in the home that most symbolizes transitions.

GETTING THROUGH
THE GETTING-USED-TO STAGE

We shall hardly notice in a year or two.
You can get accustomed to anything.

—Edna St. Vincent Millay

"*I*t's unbelievable the primitive feelings that are aroused by rapid change," writer Sheila Ballantyne points out, and rightly so. Which is why, when change occurs, Mother Providence hits the cosmic Pause button for a sacred time-out. Think of it as a way to recalibrate the speed with which we're chasing after our days. With any change in our circumstances there's new information to assimilate, emotional wounds to lick, confusion to sort, closets to clear, forms to fill out. There are new connections to make, wisdom to glean, truth to be revealed, forgiveness to be considered, mail to forward. But above all, there's gratitude to be offered for a safe deliverance from the Past before Spirit stamps our letters of transit to the Future.

"Transition is the way that we all come to terms with change," observes the psychologist William Bridges, a pioneer in the study of personal and business transitions. "Without transition, a change is mechanical, superficial, empty. If transition does not occur or if it is begun but aborted, people end up (mentally and emotionally) back where they started, and the change doesn't work. In spite of the new boss (or the new house or the new baby), nothing is really different."

Tell that to the frantic woman screaming for "closure" before the ink is dry on her divorce papers or the boxes are loaded on the van.

BACK TO THE FUTURE

You start out with one thing, end up with another,
and nothing's like it used to be, not even the future.

—Rita Dove

"Life has a way of bringing you back to places you thought you had left for good," William Bridges concedes with the irony, wisdom, and grace that only come when you suddenly discover you're circling back upon yourself. Or, as the poet T.S. Eliot so aptly put it, we arrive back where we started from, startled with astonishment that we "know the place for the first time."

The author of the groundbreaking book *Transitions: Making Sense of Life's Changes*, William Bridges found himself numb with grief and blindsided with shock 17 years later, after the death of his wife of 37 years, Mondi, from breast cancer. The couple had been on an emotional roller coaster for two years, but just when Mondi began to enjoy a particularly good remission, the cancer reappeared with a vengeance. After a wonderful month of relief and the renewal of hope, she had died. William Bridges felt not only bereft but purposeless, unable to help himself. "All the things that I had written about transition—the very things that people had said were so helpful to them—now felt strangely unreal to me. I wondered, *How could I ever have tried to pass myself off as an expert on transition?* I felt now that my words had totally failed to match in depth the *experience* of actually being in transition."

If a change is deep, the ripples of transition can be far-reaching, much like the reverberations of an earthquake are often more powerful than the initial rupture of the earth. William Bridges explains that a person can feel not only that "piece of reality gone, but that everything that had seemed to be reality was simply an enchantment. With the spell broken, life can look so differently that we hardly recognize it."

Or ourselves. Consider the aftershocks at either extreme of life's spectrum—losing your home in a flood or winning the lottery. Both events strip you of the familiar. Whether the change of clothes you put on comes from an emergency shelter or from a chic boutique you never felt welcome in before, the result is the same. We do not feel or look like ourselves. Even if we still answer to our names, we begin a wrenching process of separating from our previous identities. Think of it as psychic identity theft. We've been snatched, mind and body, from all that was customary, from the person we were just yesterday. The only entity that knows what's going on is your Soul, and when was the last time you had a good long chat with Her?

"The days of our lives vanish utterly, more insubstantial than if they had been invented," the English novelist Penelope Lively tells us. "Fiction can seem more enduring than reality."

THE WORDS REMEMBER WHEN

*Marvelous Truth, confront us
at every turn,
in every guise…*

—Denise Levertov

When I read something I'm in the process of writing and suddenly begin to weep, I know that I'm getting close to the Marvelous Truth. Inadvertently my subconscious scrawl has hit a psychic sciatic nerve and I've no choice but to go on. "The line of words fingers your own heart" is how Annie Dillard describes the process. "It invades arteries, and enters the heart on a flood of breath; it presses the moving rims of thick valves; it palpates the dark muscle … feeling for something, it knows not what."

As I knead my own nerve slowly, I chance upon a gnarled ganglia from the past—suppressed memories, calcified regrets, shards of remorse, a cyst of shame—entangled and embedded in a hard, painful knot, hidden deeply in my heart's cavity. I tap the keys, my prose probing too close for comfort, much the way a doctor taps her fingers upon the body to sense the condition of an organ through sound. Something I've not been ready to acknowledge, some reckoning I've been resisting is struggling to be heard. The Words appearing on the page insist that attention *MUST* be paid to transitions, the earthly sweet hereafter—in particular, to the fact that women like you and me ignore them because we misguidedly think we haven't the time to squander in "processing" life-changing events. Then we wonder why we end up feeling and behaving like psychic refugees— depressed, disoriented, and displaced even when living in a home worthy of *Architectural Digest*.

It's time to ransom the lives of those neglected women. It's time to ransom ourselves. The women who cringe from the mistakes they've made to have it all or who cower from the chances they shunned in order to play it safe. The women who spent their whole lives creating a designer showcase, now being enjoyed, perhaps, by a second, younger wife. The women *beyond* nervous breakdowns, the ones stashing prescription drugs, empty sherry bottles, shoe boxes, credit card receipts, cookie dough ice cream tubs.

What about women under house arrest, praying to wake up in the Witness Protection Program rather than pretend for one more day that living in a slum of self-sloth is okay? How about those gals who'd rather slop down the deck on a one-way passage to the Congo than serve up another piece of perfection pie? Don't forget the media-addicted women who rearrange every detail of their lives to the dictates of their favorite domestic goddess or glossy magazines. What about the women who have lost *everything* through death or disaster, or those living with the secret dread that tomorrow they will, because they're drowning in debt, disillusion, and despair?

The way a woman *feels* about her home reflects every bit of this emotional baggage. It is what is *felt* in a home that nurtures a woman's heart or shatters her soul. How can I help you come to grips with how you feel every time you go into one of the rooms of your home—what's heart-rending as well as heart-warming; what's hidden, what's struggling to be acknowledged, what's staring you in the face? Perhaps by learning this lesson room by room in my own home. I know it's my job to help you to see, to understand, that *it only looks like a pile of dirty laundry;* let me remember this too, as I sort the clothes or wipe down the counter. Above all, may I be blessed with the awareness that I want so much for you; when creating the House of Belonging, it's more Interior Vision the Soul longs for than interior design.

I see that I have reached the moment that inevitably occurs in each book I write. I call it "the Turning"—the point of no return. It's now much more painful to stand behind, refusing to cross the mystical, transformative threshold than to take the leap. It's now more painful to conceal than it is to reveal what Spirit is requesting of this book. Heaven is giving me a Divine "Heads up, babe." To answer this call means that my daily round is about to get reshuffled big-time. This transformation will change me personally; if you continue reading it, it will change you too. Go ahead, sweetie, I don't blame you, close the book, if you can. Avoid the Marvelous Truth. You don't have to come where I must go. Don't feel you have to finish what you've started.

This time.

CHANGE OF HEART

What would happen if one woman told the truth
about her life? The world would split open.

—Muriel Rukeyser

I've always welcomed change with about as much enthusiasm as the brick wall greets the wrecking ball. Endings? Don't do them. Endings can be so tortuously strung out, messy, untidy, fraught; so excruciatingly painful to witness, let alone endure. "Ah, the relationships [situations, circumstances] we get into just to get out of the ones we are not brave enough to say are over," Julia Phillips confesses.

Parting is much more my style. Polished. Polite. Sleek. No frayed edges showing. Well-groomed. I've been known to walk away with only the clothes on my back and my desk not cleared, which means I've become an expert on starting over from scratch. And transitions? Well, up until now I haven't just resisted virtually every transition thrust upon me, I've been a conscientious objector.

You see, transitions are about finishing what we started. Emotionally, physically, intellectually, financially, spiritually. Tying off those loose ends; well, at least knotting them. Transitions are about accepting responsibility for your choices, especially those you didn't know you were making at the time. But transitions are also about moving towards something that presumably can be better.

It hasn't escaped my notice that I wrote about women and choices in *Something More* instead of honoring the transitions that had resulted from a series of cataclysmic changes in both my personal and professional life the year before. In a mere 12 months I'd gone from being an obscure freelancer to best-selling author; a wife of 18 years to a divorcee; a woman who'd had to ask her husband for a housekeeping check of $250 every two weeks to depositing a check of her own for $1 million; a woman who lived in a house she hated on sight to buying one she loved; a woman who worked from home, scheduling her day around the car pool, to having a staff of six, with drivers to take her wherever her assistant said she needed to go.

And I turned 50.

Yes, on reflection, I think it would have been very helpful to have understood the significance of honoring life's transitions. Or even to have admitted I was going through them.

CLAIMING WHAT'S YOURS

You need to claim the events of your life to make yourself yours. When you truly possess all you have been and done, which may take some time, you are fierce with reality.

—Florida Pier Scott-Maxwell

*I*t takes a long time to understand the difference between letting go and moving on, especially if you try to bypass the transitions following life-altering change. Most women believe we can avoid transitions by becoming very busy. "Waiting, done at really high speeds, will frequently look like something else," observes Carrie Fisher hopefully. It's called multitasking. How often do we use the congestion and sheer occupation of our days to anesthetize ourselves against emotion, thought, and action? When I make myself busy and permit the activities swirling around me to grab my attention, I tell myself over and over that I can't think *today* about the choices I should be making or mourn what my heart is begging my brain to remember. Call it the Scarlett Syndrome. *I'll think about that tomorrow. I'll grieve over that tomorrow. After all, tomorrow is another day.* "Life must go on," Edna St. Vincent Millay wrote. "I forget just why."

MORE'S THE PITY

There is no sin punished more implacably by nature than the sin of resistance to change.

—Anne Morrow Lindbergh

I think the more details I learn about Anne Morrow Lindbergh's life (1906-2001), the more compelling and emblematic she becomes. However, I love her all the more for appearing to live so gracefully between the lines of her beautiful but despairingly poetic prose. The anguish of her baby's kidnapping and murder, and then the privacy invasion that had to be the first of our modern era, are well-known. Lesser known was her turbulent relationship with her husband, Charles, "the most worshipped man in the world," who in later years became a lightning rod for controversy. His participation in the isolationist "America First" movement prior to World War II, his several visits to

Germany and friendly meetings with Nazi leaders, and his determination in 1939 to persuade his countrymen to stay out of the war caused him to be castigated by President Franklin D. Roosevelt and barred him from serving his country once America did enter the war. The American public that had idolized Lucky Lindy turned on him ferociously. His disgrace must have crushed her.

Then there was the vicious savaging of her first volume of poems, *The Unicorn and Other Poems,* which followed close upon the hurrah of her best-seller *Gift From the Sea.* For the rest of her writing career, she would publish only one more poem. For anyone who has put herself out there creatively, professionally, or even in our everyday worlds, this footnote reveals legions about the risks we take: Is it worth sharing ourselves, intimately, honestly, and generously, only to be made to feel diminished and dishonored by it?

I sense that this cherished writer— appalled that women looked upon her as a role model—had as much difficulty dealing with life's transitions as the traumas that made them so necessary.

"The space is scribbled on; the time has been filled. There are so few empty pages in my engagement pad, or empty hours in the day, or empty rooms in my life in which to stand alone and find myself," she revealed towards the end of her memoir, *Gift From the Sea.* "Too many activities, and people, and things. Too many worthy activities, valuable things, and interesting people. For it is not merely the trivial which clutters our lives but the important as well."

Anne never believed that there was a sympathetic audience for her heartfelt ambivalence. "Many women are content with their lives as they are. They manage amazingly well, far better than I.... With envy and admiration, I [observe] the porcelain perfection of their smoothly ticking days..." She confessed to the page: "The life I have chosen as wife and mother entrains a whole caravan of complications. It involves a house in the suburbs and either household drudgery or household help which wavers between scarcity and nonexistence for most of us. It involves food and shelter; meals, planning, marketing, bills, and making the ends meet in a thousand ways. It involves not only the butcher, the baker, the candlestick maker, but countless other experts to keep my modern house with its modern 'simplications' (electricity, plumbing, refrigerator, gas-stove, oil-burner, dish-wash, radios, cars, and numerous other labor-saving devices) functioning properly. It involves health; doctors, dentists, appointments, medicine, cod-liver oil, vitamins, trips to the drugstore. It involves education, spiritual, intellectual, physical; schools, school conferences, car-pools, extra trips for basket-ball or orchestra practice, tutoring, camps, camp equipment and transportation. It involves clothes, shopping, laundry, cleaning, mending, letting skirts down and sewing buttons on, or finding someone else to do it. It involves friends, my husband's, my children's, my own, and endless arrangements together; letters, invitations, telephone calls and transportation hither and yon ... My mind reels with it."

Yes, her mind was reeling—just like yours, just like mine.

Certainly no time today for contemplating life transitions. "Can one make the future a substitute for the present?" she asks. Not until we make peace with our past, I'm sadder and sorrier to say than I hope, dear Reader, you'll ever be.

SLEIGHT OF HANDS

Women are like tricks by sleight of hand,
Which, to admire, we should not understand.

—William Congreve

Remember when you were little and played on the jungle gym? Jungle gym bars are perfect to help you understand the difference between letting go and moving on. You're ten years old, you're holding onto the high bar with both hands and all your might. Your hands are gripping the bar, they're turning white at the knuckles, your arms are aching, and your body is getting heavier, pulling you down. Now your hands are getting sweaty and your grip begins to slip and slide, and then, before too long, you let go. Plop. You're lying in a heaving, exhausted dusty heap on the ground. The recess alarm bell rings. You get up, dust yourself off, and start walking back to the classroom, laughing with your friends. That's moving on. You hold fast, let go, fall down or apart, then get up and move on. The holding on/letting go struggle is passive (although you feel it with all your might) but it's inertia, because it's getting you nowhere. In contrast, picking yourself up off the playground or putting your life back together after a crisis is passionate, because it's forward motion. One tiny step, one tumultuous turning.

A NET FOR CATCHING DAYS

> *It is not the conscious changes made in their lives by men and women—a new job, a new town, a divorce—which really shape them, like the chapter headings in a biography, but a long, slow mutation of emotion, hidden, all-penetrative.*

—Nadine Gordimer

Waiting is passive. We wait for our nails to dry, our name to be called, or a recorded message to connect us to a live person; we wait for the delivery or an important call; we wait for the traffic to move; to pay for our groceries; to catch a bus. Waiting is surrendering a block of time to someone else, or to a schedule, which is not of our own making, and may not even be in our own best interests.

I once wrote that waiting was the soul of the Divine Scheme of things. *Au contraire. Pardonnez-moi.*

I know now that transitions are passionate phases in our lives, not passive ones. During transitions we grow into the person we're meant to become, even if we don't know who she is right now. Transitions can be painful, difficult, messy, and downright scary at times, but if we just keep moving, they don't have to be horrendous. Certain change in our lives, such as losing someone or something we loved, can be devastating for years afterwards; but ultimately it's our resistance to the transition that sabotages our healing.

Think of transitions as rites of passage, as well as sacred right-of-ways. We edge down a darkened corridor slowly until we can feel the light switch. There's spiritual electricity waiting to be turned on during transitions; a sublime synchronicity getting us to the right place at the right time, *if we just keep moving.* But we don't. We stop, play dead, and hope that change and transition will find another victim. As a strategy for survival, it's pretty flawed. Put your head in the sand and your butt becomes a beautiful target for buckshot.

After my husband, Jonnie, and I married last year, we did not have time for a proper honeymoon because of work commitments. (It's always something and usually it sounds reasonable.) Instead, we took a few days away, spending most of that time passed out from the exhaustion of the wedding. On the last night before we came home, I wrenched my knee in the most stupid way possible—by tripping on an open suitcase lying on the floor. It was right in front of me, but I wasn't looking where I was going.

At a time when I should have been leaping for joy with my new life, for weeks I could barely hobble. It was as if my mind and body literally stopped me in my tracks, as if to say: "Look, you can't go back and you won't go forward, so you're going nowhere." Fair enough, because that's exactly what had happened. Why wasn't I reveling in my glorious new beginning with the love of my life? A gorgeous, intelligent, funny, sexy, amazing, incredible man after years of loneliness? It's because I wouldn't allow myself the time to transition into being a wife again, as well as into becoming a stepmother to two teenage boys.

Secretly I was grieving over the loss of the life I'd shared for the last seven years with my only child—two chicks together—as well as worrying about losing my hard-won independence. I felt as if something had died. Well, hadn't it? Perhaps the wedding feast always follows fast upon the heart's wake, not just for Hamlet's mother, but for all women who marry, especially those of us who marry later in life and find ourselves creating new family configurations. As we all negotiate new boundaries, take steps forward and back, there's bound to be as much confusion as joy. We need to be brave enough to invite our contradictions to the same party as our new commitments. If we do, we become like the woman Ellen Glasgow described in her 1925 novel, *Barren Ground,* who finally realizes that "the strong impulses which had once wrecked her happiness were the forces that had enabled her to rebuild her life out of the ruins."

LETTING HERSELF GO

Something that required the best of us has ended.
You will miss it.

—Anne Wilson Schaef

"Why is letting go so hard?" asks William Bridges, surely for all of us. "This is a puzzling question, especially if we have been looking forward to a change. It is frightening to discover that some part of us is still holding onto what we used to be, for it makes us wonder whether the change was in fact a bad idea. Can it be that the old thing was somehow (and in spite of everything we thought we knew) right for us and the new thing wrong?" Consider "the full-time mother who finally decides to break the narrow bounds of housecleaning and carpooling by taking a part-time job, or the bored office worker who gets a chance to join the staff of a newly formed company—these people hardly expect to find their old roles difficult to shed. And the person who has been estranged from parents or siblings for years won't expect to be profoundly shaken by their deaths. How can we feel a 'loss' when we marry after years of loneliness, or receive an inheritance after struggling to make ends meet, or achieve fame after a career spent trying to make it?"

One of the reasons that people "resist transitions is that it sets up *resonance* between the present and painful experiences in the past," William Bridges continues. "It is as though the later experience of loss *vibrates* and sets other, older losses on the same wavelength, vibrating sympathetically. A person who lost a parent during childhood, for example, is likely to be especially vulnerable to the ending of an adult relationship…. People whose lives came apart once because of a difficult physical move that took them away from everyone they cared about are likely to find subsequent moves upsetting. And people with childhood experiences of profound failure—the kind that leave you feeling worthless and hopeless—can be especially vulnerable to experiences in which their sense of personal worth or adequacy is challenged.... It is no accident that it is the pain triggered off by transition that often leads people into psychotherapy, or that one of the tasks they face in psychotherapy is to disentangle present realities (which may be painful enough in their own right) from the remembered traumas of the past."

A FRONT HALL TO ENTHRALL

Each room contains a mythic universe.

—Robert Sardello

A few years ago I had a beautiful, large, luxurious pre-war apartment on one of the most glorious boulevards in New York City. The walls were thick, the ceilings high, the windows enormous, and the rent exorbitant, but I justified paying more per month than I had earned annually as a freelancer for the previous 20 years as a well-deserved perk of my new, successful life. This was also not in the least way sensible, or what you'd expect from the woman who wrote *Simple Abundance*. It was, in fact, reckless. Maybe that's why I did it. But the apartment represented something far more than shelter: To my eye it was what success looked like.

But that was then and this is now. Sometimes we must go on living longer than we'd like with the choices we made before we knew better. Honoring transitions that come after cataclysmic change is how we maintain our equilibrium and preserve what's left of our sanity and savings account.

On the plus side of life's ledger, I had more fun decorating that space than I've ever had, before or since. The furnishings were elegant, sophisticated, comfortable, witty, and sexy. The entire apartment was lovely, but the foyer was enthralling. Think of space as foreplay. Here, let me open the door and welcome you in. First you'll see a huge Art Deco mirror hanging over a breathtaking golden walnut burl wood credenza, circa 1930. Imagine the Latin film siren Dolores Del Rio's curves, shoulders, and décolletage had been transformed into an *Art Moderne* cocktail cabinet. Orson Welles declared her "the most beautiful woman in the world" (she also was his wife for a tempestuous time) and this sideboard was her incarnation.

The guided tour continues. On the opposite wall, leading into a proper drawing room (far too grand to be labeled "living"), was an immense oil painting by the Irish artist Sir John Lavery (1856–1941) called *The Sunbathers*. It depicts, in "glorious Technicolor," two starlets in strapless bathing suits lounging on a Mexican rug and throw pillows with the shadow of the artist himself, painting under a large umbrella. It's bright, happy, boisterous. A sensuous bravura of color—orange, yellow, red, blue—that makes you smile just to gaze upon it. After a lifetime of painting perfectly poised English society portraits in patrician gray and black, Lavery did my painting at the age of 81 during a visit to Palm Springs, California, following the death of his beloved wife, Hazel. It marked a new beginning at the end of his life.

What astonishes me is that the last time *The Sunbathers* was seen publicly was at the Paris Salon of 1938; and then war came and many famous art works disappeared from view. To think of all that passion—Lavery's stunning tour de force—hidden for 60 years stirred something deep within me. When it came up for auction seven decades later, I vowed it would be mine. And so it came to pass.

Few places in the world have ever gifted me with as much profound pleasure as crossing the threshold of this apartment; every entrance took my breath away; the memory of it aches. Whenever I walked into that foyer, I blossomed into every woman I'd ever hoped to be. The siren in every film, the hostess of every sought-after soirée. The transition was hypnotic and powerful. To tell the truth now, I couldn't believe it was mine; I couldn't understand how I was living there. I wonder if that isn't one of the reasons that it's no longer mine. It's hard to hold on to what we don't believe we deserve.

The real problem, however, was that it was really a very expensive pied-à-terre, because I actually *lived* out of several suitcases in New York, Washington, and London. The apartment remained regrettably empty for lengthy stretches; in the first year I rented, I'd be surprised if I spent more than six weeks there. I know, I know—Bad girl.

I was going to let it go when my lease came up for renewal (with a hefty rent increase, naturally). Instead, I held my breath and *chose* to stay. The selection of that word is very precise (although up until this moment I have managed beautifully to squirm away from this reality). I *chose* to spend my money this way, even if I was oblivious to the implications. Decisions like these are coma choices, followed by amnesia awakenings. When you finally come to, you say, "I don't know what I was thinking." That's because you *weren't* thinking, toots. Calculating, maybe. Taking a flyer on the margin. Trying to sneak under the Soul's radar. It's a form of spiritual gambling, really. But not thinking. Not really doing anything bad, babe. Just not making the best choice for you, or for me.

How about a little refresher on the spiritual gift of choice? It's so convenient to forget. Well, at least it was for me. Many women don't think of choice as a gift of grace; we think choices are burdens to be endured, not embraced. (And if you don't believe me, how many nights have you eaten chicken this week? What's your work uniform look like? How long has "Nude" been your lipstick color? When you go out for a drink can your friends automatically guess if you'll order Chardonnay or Merlot?)

You get my drift. We think of choice the same way we think of transitions. But the price of avoidance is high. You may not realize it or want to believe it (neither do I when it comes to recalling the apartment), but your life at this exact moment is a direct result of choices you made once upon a time. Thirty minutes or 30 years ago.

Our choices are either conscious or unconscious. Conscious is best. Conscious choice is creative—the heart of authenticity. Unconscious choice is destructive—the heel of self-abuse. Unconscious choice is how we end up living other people's lives in apartments we can't afford.

"The most common despair is ... not choosing or willing to be oneself," the Danish philosopher Søren Kierkegaard warns us, "[but] the deepest form of despair is to choose to be another than oneself."

That's the part about choices I wish I'd remembered.

"It's when we're given choice that we sit with the gods and design ourselves," writer Dorothy Gilman sighs. Oh yes, when we know that this choice will cost us—physically, emotionally, financially, spiritually, psychologically—and are prepared to pick up the check, then choice is priceless. Unfortunately, there's no sure way of knowing the tab until we've lived the choice; we can't see in advance whether the choice was a wise or wrong one. But at least it was ours to make. We also can't really know where a choice will take us, although we might sense its direction. We're torn between the agonizing shoulds and shouldn'ts. I love the way the English writer Jeanette Winterson describes our dilemma: "I have a theory that every time you make an important choice, the part of you left behind continues the other life you could have had."

So you gather as much information as you can. You weigh your options. You ponder the possibilities. You brood. You probe the probabilities with your best friend. You ask your heart. You pray for guidance. Then you land on your feet. You live your choice. You don't look back for a long time. Eventually, with hindsight, you'll glance back and see which

S A R A H   B A N   B R E A T H N A C H

it was, a wise or wrong choice. Spirit asks nothing more.
Neither should you or I.

But wrong choices should never be confused with *bad*
choices. Bad choices—and I have made some doozies—happen when we embark on sinuous stretches of self-destruc-
tion, usually with a smile or something to prove. My head
wants to declare that gorgeous New York apartment to be a
bad choice, slap my knuckles with a ruler, and say, "So,
there, missy!" but I think that what was so bad about it was
the furtive way I went about it. I did not ask my heart or a
pal for advice. I did not ponder and I certainly did not pray.
Why? Because on the deepest intuitive level I knew I
shouldn't even have been entertaining the thought of this
two-year renewal. However, I loved what this apartment
represented—that I'd made it against all the odds and the
money was mine to spend however I damn well pleased. So
I closed my eyes. This way, I could honestly say that I never
saw disaster coming.

LET IT BE

Many a truth is the result of an error.
—Marie von Ebner-Eschenbach

In September 2001 my daughter, Kate, was starting New
York University, and while she would be living in a
dorm downtown, she wanted to have a "home" base uptown
for weekends. I couldn't have been more thrilled. Now I had
a legitimate reason to be a libertine.

In fact, I had moved her into her dorm just before Labor Day. My plans were to return to England to finish *Romancing the Ordinary*. Originally, I was going to leave the following day but something made me change my flight; this was a huge adjustment for her and I wanted to make sure she was settled before I returned to Newton's Chapel.

I had so many errands to do that gorgeous Tuesday morning. So busy. I was about to whiz out the door when Kate called. She'd just left her dorm as the first plane buzzed low over Fifth Avenue and then flew into the World Trade Center. It was 8:50 a.m., and she could see the gaping hole and smoke from the street. I couldn't comprehend what she was telling me so I immediately switched on the television; they were reporting it as a freak air traffic control accident. I told Katie, in that reassuring tone women have always used as a crisis begins to take shape, ears half-cocked, that everything would be all right and she should just go to class. Within minutes I realized that things would probably never be "all right" again.

After her classes were suspended, Kate was walking back to her dorm with her roommates when the second tower collapsed in front of them. They fell on the ground screaming, covering their heads from the horror. Like millions of other people around the world I watched the unthinkable unfold on television; I've no idea how long my hand was at my mouth, but long enough for this response to have become my psychic default gesture. For six frantic hours I tried to reach my daughter on her cell phone; around 4 p.m. she rang me. Thank God! She was walking uptown and was about 20 blocks away.

The sight of Katie as she stepped into the apartment foyer was my Second Coming. The hugs, the kisses, the tears, the relief. The *feel* of her in my arms. The smell of loss that clung to her clothing. The taste of salt on her dusty cheeks. The sense of overwhelming gratitude, laced with guilt.

The dorm had been evacuated. Kate brought her three roommates with her; I told all the girls to just leave their backpacks on the floor, to go now, wash their hands and faces, and then call their families to let them know they were safe. I went into the kitchen, put sandwiches on plates, and poured wine. I said more prayers. Blessed was I among women. How grateful I was to have this apartment, uptown and out of harm's way. So healing, so able to hold us together. Forgive me my happiness. If I were given the chance to do it all again, not knowing then what I do now, I would make the same choice today. It was worth every penny. Every tear shed. Every regret. Every reckoning.

So maybe it wasn't so wrong after all?

Sure it was. But it was best damn wrong choice I've ever made in my life. And that makes it okay.

Finally.

WHO KNOWS WHERE OR WHEN

On the threshold the entire past and the endless future rush to meet one another.

—Gunilla Norris

Y ou've heard the Deeper Vibration too. I know you have. That's because Divine Change is vibrational. We've only kidded ourselves into believing that change appears out of nowhere. There is nothing erratic, irrational, and random about change. As regular as the ebb and flow of the tides, the recurring sequence of the four seasons, the monthly phases of the moon, menstruation, and menopause, and the daily progression from day into night, change can be counted on. And if you allow yourself to be still enough, you can even hear change approaching.

Very often change arrives softly, a gentle whisper, meant to soothe our misgivings, even inspire us to begin to make those subtle course corrections in certain situations in our lives. We don't. So change becomes a recurring theme in our lives, a pulsating riff, the same issue wrapped in different circumstances. For example, in one month, you lose your keys, your job, your lover, your wallet, your lease. Hang on, what's happening here? What situation in life have you been dragging your heels about; what are you ducking that you should have ended long ago? Or what don't you believe you deserve? What is it you fear someone will take away? Security. Safety. Serenity. Love. Money. Health. Happiness. Your husband. Home. Everything?

Loss is trying to get your attention before Change gets into town.

The medical-intuitive Caroline Myss, a pioneer in the field of energy medicine and human consciousness, tells us that when we know we are supposed to move on or out of a situation that is stunting our soul growth and we consciously refuse to do so because the uncharted terror of choice and change scares us, a celestial clock starts ticking. "If you're getting directions, 'Move on with your life, let go of something.' Then do it. Have the courage to do it. This is the way it is. When you get guidance to let go of something, it's sort of like a time warning that says, 'You have ten days left. After that, your angel's going to do it.' So the desire to hold on is not going to stop the process of change."

I'll never forget my reaction when I got that message while listening to Caroline Myss's audiotape *Spiritual Madness: The Necessity of Meeting God in Darkness.* Isn't that interesting? I thought, I wonder if she's right? Ten days later, my life was lying in smithereens around my ankles and I was shaking my head, terrified and incredulous.

Who's wailing on the saxophone outside *your* bedroom window at 4 a.m? Slam the window, close the drapes, put the pillow over your head. Miss the beat, but, baby, it still goes on.

But what if we choose to change? Greet its arrival. As Christina Baldwin reminds us, "When you're stuck in a spiral, to change all aspects of the spin you need only to change one thing."

What if you were willing to finish what you start—one task at a time—just for one day? Have you any idea of the sheer relief and enormous accomplishment you would feel at the end of such day? The burden that would be lifted from your shoulders?

What if today you stopped running? Running scared. Running away. Running in place. Running in circles. Running interference. Running amok. Running on empty. Right now. Let's just stop. Instead of running anymore, let's say a prayer:

HEART REFLECTIONS:
THE BELOVED ASKS FOR THE GIFT OF DIVINE COMPLETION

P iercer of Doubt and Kindler of Courage, bless this woman, my dearly beloved Reader. Thank you for your clarity and compassion. Thank you for Divine Completion. We ask for the gift of Grace today to finish whatever we started and abandoned so long ago, to let go of the ghosts that harass our days and haunt our nights. We ask to return in safety and strength to the ruins of our regrets, to ransom what can be rescued and release what begs for rest. Help us, we pray, to make the transition from fear to faith, to make peace with our past, so we might live this day with the astonishing wonder of our first and the wisdom of our last. Encourage us to claim all the events of our lives so that we might become fierce with our own exquisite, incomparable reality. Shape, from all our sighs, a Shelter of Serenity; design, with all that delights, a Dwelling place of Contentment. Return to us the repose of our ravished souls.

Grant this woman safe passage, we pray, from her turbulent Endings, through Divine Transition to her tenuous, but true New Beginnings. Please lead my cherished friend, Your Beloved, to the threshold of her own understanding. Welcome this woman to her House of Belonging. Come, celebrate her Home.

DO TRY THIS AT HOME:
ACCUSTOMED TO HER PACE

When you walk into your home at the end of a grueling day, do the stresses and strains fall away, or does clutter and disharmony add further to your headaches? Is your home the nurturing haven it should be, or is it a continuation of the chaos of the outside world?

—Beverly Pagram

In time travel movies, the Traveler must cross supernatural thresholds fraught with uncertainty and danger between the past and possibility, between the present and futility. Actually we do too. Between here and there. Between what was and what is. Between what should be and what isn't. Between our front and back doors.

Entrances have always been sacred portals to the sublime, though this probably wasn't your first thought after squeezing out of the car in the darkened garage, shopping bags held aloft as you deftly leapt over the opened bag of cat litter (nice one!), upturned rake, paint cans, and bicycle, before groping your way past the freezer and into the laundry room.

Making an entrance with our usual flair?

"Transition is a key factor in spiritual experience," the architect Anthony Lawlor reminds us in his luminous book, *A Home for the Soul: A Guide for Dwelling with Spirit and Imagination.* "The threshold marks the boundary of transition, the line which must be crossed to enter new realms of experience." The French have a wonderful expression for this threshold encounter—*le foyer*—which means not only the entry space surrounding the door where one enters a home but the pleasures of the "hearth" to be found there— an intimate invitation for guests to relax and make themselves feel "at home." And while we all extend that greeting when company calls, what feeling welcomes us every day?

For instance, let me ask you again, as I did earlier in this chapter: Which door do you use to enter your home? If you live in a house, you have at least two or three; chances are that the one you use regularly is the one nearest to the kitchen, where you can easily drop your shopping bags, briefcase, coat, purse, shoes, umbrellas, and the like.

"Today, it's customary to enter our houses through the back door, or the cellar door, which is nearest the garage— convenient for carrying in groceries and other bundles, yes, but not exactly a gracious way to re-freshen our spirits after long hours away from home," the writer and interior designer Alexandra Stoddard muses in *Creating a Beautiful Home*. "Perhaps it's because we've gotten away from putting our front entrances to daily use that so many of them feel stiff and awkward. If nothing else, I think it's time to rethink the daily pattern of entering our real lives through the back door. We should begin to enjoy the full bounty of our houses every day."

So what's a practical woman to do? You need the ease of the back door, you say? Not as much as you need the transition from warp speed to a slow crawl, which a proper entrance to your home provides. What's more, when we rigorously maintain a public versus private division we unconsciously transform our houses into habitats instead of shelters for the Soul. Saving the best entryway for guests is another way of self-slighting—a wily disregard for the dignity of our own presence, as disrespectful and diminishing as reserving the best china and table linens only for visitors. The important link for women between transitions and foyers is to recognize they're both passageways—one emotional, the other physical—to help us adapt to change, whether it's a new job or coming home from one.

We must also be willing to reconsider our personal velocity, the relentless hyperdrive with which we propel ourselves throughout the day, multistarting so many tasks but rarely finishing any of them except by fluke. I hate to be the one to bring this up, but the appalling psychic imbalance most of us call "real life" is a hallucinogenic joke conjured up for the convenience of the rest of the world. Lurching from one task to another like zombies, cramming yesterday's exhaustion into tomorrow's obligations, is not an ordinary life; it's lunacy. There's much to be said about living each day as if it were our last on earth, but the sharp point of that wisdom is to *enjoy* your last day here, not to try to get "caught up" before you check out. And if you won't listen to me, try to hear the truth in what Anne Morrow Lindbergh wrote in 1955:

"What a circus act we women perform every day of our lives. It puts the trapeze artist to shame. Look at us. We run a tight rope daily, balancing a pile of books on the head. Baby-carriage, parasol, kitchen chair, still under control. Steady now! This is not the life of simplicity but the life of multiplicity.... It does not bring grace; it destroys the soul. And this is not only true of my life, I am forced to conclude; it is the life of millions of women in America. I stress America, because today, the American woman more than any other has the privilege of choosing such a life."

We *choose* this madness.

You might ask, "How does any woman driven to distraction rid herself of debilitating dizzy spells? They're such time-wasters!" Well, if you see your doctor for a proper, personal diagnosis, you'll probably be told to slow down. Take it down a notch, one day at a time. Besides an intravenous drip of Bach's *Rescue Remedy* (my idea), I'm only allowed to concentrate on one task at a time. No more talking on the phone and opening the mail simultaneously. No making the bed while brushing my teeth. No emptying the dishwasher while sautéing the mushrooms. No chopping the onions while listening to the news. No eating while watching television. No working in bed—only sleeping or cuddling permitted. Yikes! It's enough to make a grown woman *stop* screaming. I don't quite know what to do with myself.

I've also created a ceremony for winding down when I come home from work to make the transition from working to relaxing—not an easy adjustment for a workaholic. What do you usually do as soon as you walk through the door in the evening? Glance through the mail? Listen to your phone messages? Check your e-mail? Flick on the evening news? Read the paper? Do you feel disappointed if nothing urgent is happening? Oddly, now that communications have become instantaneous, it's incredibly difficult to wean ourselves from the sensory overload of the outside world. But if we don't, who will?

Give yourself the indulgence of a half hour spent downshifting into private time. Have something luxurious to change into when you're at home; lay it out on the end of your made bed before you leave for work. Take time as you change your clothes, freshen your makeup, comb your hair, and spritz on some lovely cologne that you only wear at home. Now put the kettle on, or pour a glass of something delicious and refreshing, caress your pet, water the plants. Play some special music that induces serenity or smiles and listen to it only when you come home in the evening; piano nocturnes are very restorative, the reassuring rhythm of individual notes blending into a beautiful harmony. Now putter around the different rooms of your home. Can you go out to the backyard and cut a small bouquet of flowers? Could you bring some flowers home with you? Enjoy arranging them. Can you hear a clock ticking in your home? If your heart races, a sure way to calm down is to heed the soothing rhythm of an old clock.

After you've reconnected to everything living in your environment (and that does include you), get the evening meal started, and when it's underway and doesn't need close attention, sort the mail (next to a wastepaper basket), immediately tossing the junk into the trash without opening it. Should you be so fortunate as to have some personal letters, save them until you can give these rare pleasures the attention they deserve. Should you be even more fortunate to share your home with charming company, draw them out in conversation and really listen to how their day was. Make eye contact, give them a smile, and most important, hug them. In our daily to-ing and fro-ing, we lose track of how much we keep life and love at arm's length.

While we're at it, here's another radical thought: Determine one set time for when you'll check your e-mail and another for when you'll answer it, plus a time to return phone calls (preferably tomorrow). If you do only one new thing this month, strive to make your evenings at home as personal and relaxing as possible.

Obviously, it takes a bit of time to become accustomed to this pace. I won't pretend that it isn't frustrating to change from multitasking to solely focusing on only one job at a time. It's new behavior, and it'll take a little while to adapt to it, but I'm giving myself the gift of time. What's more, I've started to use the front door to enter my house and the back door to exit. Now there's a step in the right direction.

NESTING INSTINCTS:
COMINGS AND GOINGS

The intrusions of the mundane become agents of the sublime.
—Lynda Sexson

Okay, let's take another look at what the rest of the world sees, but you've become blind to—your front door. A good entryway should make you feel welcome as you approach, happily anticipating entering its portals. So go outside (right now), walk up from the street to your front door, and react. Don't hold back. Is the approach neat, tidy, pretty? Or is it neglected, overgrown, in need of either some tender loving care or adoption by the neighbors? Imagine for a moment that someone you really admire walked past your house and saw you on the front step and said, "Hi! So this is where you live."

Whoa. Calm down. This is only pretend. Why have you suddenly become a shrinking violet? Maybe you can't overhaul your entry this minute, but is there something you can take down, throw away, pick up? What about a new doormat?

Replacing the burned-out bulb over the door? How about choosing (there's that word again!) two attractive and living plants (in matching pots) to replace dead stalks?

"Even the smallest Entrance Hall has plenty of room for beauty," instructed *House Beautiful* in January 1927. "Sometimes it takes quite a bit of fussing and changing things about to get a pleasing decorative effect in an entrance hall." Both inside and out.

Architect Sarah Susanka reminds us in *Home by Design: Transforming Your House into Home* that the "process of entering" not only our house but our private life within its walls begins at the street or driveway and proceeds up to the front door. "So the path between the two, as well as the place that you arrive at the front door, sets the stage for what you'll find once inside."

And what do we find? Dare we peek or is it *Bleak House*'s thoroughfare of despair? A messy catch-all of junk absentmindedly deposited on the floor or stair steps by various family members as they were just passing through? Granted, the mail, umbrellas, keys, even the dog's leash has to go somewhere, but DVDs, shoes, golf clubs, and hairbrushes belong in other rooms, preferably their owners'. When a woman is fidgety, frazzled, and highly fraught, her pretty, serene, well-ordered foyer can be a very comforting friend, indeed.

CHAPTER FOUR

NEVER CAN SAY GOOD-BYE

ON WOMEN AND STORAGE

Life changes fast.
Life changes in the instant.
You sit down to dinner and life as you know it ends.

—Joan Didion

THE ORDINARY INSTANT

*S*uddenly, inexplicably, and more often than anyone
ever suspects, life stuns us with loss. We lose a loved
one, or our job. We lose our home, or our health. Without
warning, hearts are broken, dreams are dashed, fortunes
reversed, reputations tarnished. Gone are the assumptions
that sustained us; the expectations that shaped us; the

illusions that propped us up. We feel as if life is over—and we are right. Life as we knew it *is* over. In an instant. The ordinary instant.

Whether the loss is personal, precipitated by a phone call in the middle of the night, or collective, announced during a breakfast television bulletin, *what was,* only a moment ago— serenity, sanity, security, safety, sameness—is ruthlessly snatched away or blown to smithereens. And we are left behind—bewildered, bereft, and incredulous at the horrific reality of *what is* now facing us.

In the early days after loss it's hard to imagine that anything good might come from the misery now engulfing you. You and your husband of 40 years return from visiting your adult daughter, your only child, who is in a coma at the hospital. You begin to prepare dinner, he sits down to have a scotch while you're tossing the salad; suddenly, he lifts his arm, then slumps over in his chair from a massive heart attack. A friend calls you from her doctor's office; she's just discovered she has liver cancer. She has six months. Her children are 5 and 8, and they're playing in the backyard with your kids.

The ordinary instant.

A drunk driver runs a red light. A suicide bomber takes the same bus to work as your sister. Your son wins a coveted Olympic long-distance team slot, then tells you about a strange tingling in his legs when running. Your niece and her new husband save for two years for their first-class beach honeymoon in Thailand; their suite has an ocean view; the tsunami demolishes their luxury hotel in less than a sunny, ordinary instant. One minute you're headed out to Wal-Mart to get back-to-school supplies in New Orleans and the next week your child is attending school in Houston and all you have with you are the clothes on your back.

The ordinary instant.

"Confronted with sudden disaster, we all focus on how unremarkable the circumstances were in which the unthinkable occurred, the clear blue sky from where the plane fell, the routine errand that ended on the shoulder with the car in flames, the swings where the children were playing as usual when the rattlesnake struck from the ivy," Joan Didion reflects in her haunting memoir of grief, *The Year of Magical Thinking*. Written in the year following the sudden death of her husband, writer John Gregory Dunne, in December 2003 and published just before her daughter Quintana Roo died unexpectedly in August 2005, Joan Didion ventures for all of us into the realm of the unspeakable to beautifully and courageously narrate the cartography of a heart rent asunder, a journey that we all know we must take some ordinary day. Please, God, not today.

Perhaps our lives have been turned inside out only temporarily; here and now, there's no way of knowing. Perhaps your own body has sustained an invasion: surgery, injury, illness. Chronic pain becomes habit-forming; so do the barbituates used to control the pain. Your elderly mother cannot live on her own; the insurance company won't pay the claim; a child has been suspended from school for drug dealing;

your favorite brother-in-law is indicted for insider trading. Photographs slipped through the mail slot reveal that your husband has *not* been working late at the office.

The shattered Soul sifts and sorts through plans gone awry, priorities misplaced, and promises that can no longer be kept. Devastated, our knees buckle; we stumble in the darkness, rage in anger, hurl faith across the room, abandon all hope, sob ourselves to sleep. The ordinary has been swept away, replaced by despair and uncertainty. All we know is that we are stunned, shocked, hurting, grieving, groping with too many unknowns to consider and too many contingencies to handle as we attempt in vain the great undoing of what can't be undone.

THE LONG GOOD-BYE

People have to learn sometimes not only how much the heart, but how much the head, can bear.

—Maria Mitchell

"It is easy to see the beginnings of things, and harder to see the ends," Joan Didion wrote in *Slouching Towards Bethlehem*. "I can remember now, with a clarity that makes the nerves in the back of my neck constrict, when New York began for me, but I cannot lay my finger upon the moment it ended, can never cut through the ambiguities and second starts and broken resolves to the exact place on the page where the heroine is no longer as optimistic as she once was."

I can't recall the beginning of my New York sojourn; it

happened gradually over several years starting with the publishing excursions I made in November 1988 with my literary agent, Chris Tomasino, shopping around a proposal for my first book, *Mrs. Sharp's Traditions*. Back then I'd make the trip from Maryland to New York in one day, catching the earliest Metroliner in the dark to be in the Big City by 9 a.m., watching the pennies, not wanting to be away overnight from my first-grader, but so proud of my purpose and determination to make it, which in those days was to become a published *book* author. I'd already "made it" as a journalist with a nationally syndicated column with The Washington Post Writers Group. After that the next rung on the writing ladder was a book contract with a major publisher, which I got with Simon & Schuster before Christmas that year. I remember I was baking for our annual holiday open house when there was a knock on the door; I remember being annoyed as I had to wipe my hands to answer the door. And then I remember my great surprise and delight when I was handed a gorgeous red poinsettia, beautifully wrapped. It was from my new editor, welcoming me. I remember how thrilled I was at the unexpected generous gesture and the luxuriousness of the gift—how I had to put it high on the mantel because we had three cats and poinsettias are poisonous to curious felines. I remember being so grateful and giddy. It's a happy memory. But what exactly is memory?

Women who wax lyrical will tell you memory is "the skin of life" (Elizabeth Hardwick), "the library of the soul" (Tove Ditlevsen), "a skilled seducer" (Cristina Garcia), or "what the saucer is to the cup" (Elizabeth Bowen). I think of memory as indelible photographs taken with disposable cameras but never dropped off at the drugstore for processing; by the time you get them back, years later, the moments captured on celluloid are isolated and disjointed, and you need to recall or invent a narrative to accompany them so they'll make sense. "How we remember, what we remember, and why we remember form the most personal map of our individuality," the writer Christina Baldwin tells us. Yes, I'm sure that's very true. But what is it exactly we're remembering?

Interestingly, from a scientific perspective—both medical and technological—memory is described as "storage," the capability and function of our brain (or a computer) to "save" or retain information. What's being stored are bits of encoded electromagnetic impulses arranged in specific patterns like the dot and dash messages sent out from an old Marconi ship-to-shore wireless radio. When we tie our shoelaces, drive home from work, read a book, play a card game, scramble an egg, make a pitch at a sales meeting, look for a receipt, order from a menu, book a ticket on the Internet, or travel back to where the heroine began to lose her precious optimism, this information is recalled and reassembled to help us make our way in the world.

"It is easy to forget just how much we need to remember in order to do the simplest things. We don't think of ourselves as having to remember our own names, or where we live, or how to eat or read," British writer and psychoanalyst Adam Phillips reminds us. "And yet, memory—all the skills and impressions we so carefully acquired in the past—informs much of what we do.... It is only when things begin to go wrong that we begin to notice just what it is we have been taking for granted. Our incompetence is a revelation."

THE DEATH OF THE HEART

> *Only in a house where one has learnt to be lonely does one have this solicitude for things. One's relation to them, the daily seeing or touching, begins to become love, and to lay one open to pain.*
>
> —Elizabeth Bowen

*T*he clarity with which I remember my New York ending is so acute that it's difficult for me to breathe as I write. Memories like this are vestiges of emotional battles we weren't able to fight. Maybe we were little when the war for our soul and sanity was initially waged and we couldn't defend ourselves. "Perhaps we suffered a single, mind-injuring calamity—an accident, an assault, difficult surgery, a relationship shock," Dr. Nick Baylis, Psychology Lecturer at Cambridge University explains. Or our suffering may "have been recurrent and long-term, such as years of physical or emotional bullying. A child might even be traumatized simply by being told of an incident that horrifies them, or by observing a distraught adult." Whatever the cause, we suffer what many soldiers experience after they return from combat—post-traumatic stress disorder. Twice in my life, 20 years apart, I sustained serious head injuries, and each time I had to cope both with recovering physically from the concussions, as well as the post-traumatic stress the accidents set in motion. Whatever the nature of our traumatizing experience, Nick Baylis tells us that the sensory circumstances surrounding it— the sights, sounds, smells, sensations, even tastes associated with our initial shock or heartbreak—have been lodged "like a piece of emotional shrapnel in our brain, causing us to be hypervigilant. What alarms us may not have been the most damaging element at the time of the trauma, but simply the feature that our brain happened to latch onto" for its early warning system. In other words, it's *what* we remember and the *way* we remember it.

My memory is this. It's late Friday afternoon at the end of January 2004 and I've got to catch a plane. *Come on now, you don't want to get caught up in rush hour traffic,* my personal assistant urges me. She's hurrying me along like a recalcitrant, dawdling child. I've just wandered through every room of the New York apartment in a daze, vaguely aware that all this stuff will be in storage somewhere until I can send it to England. There's barely a square inch left in tiny Newton's Chapel to take any overflow from New York. And I *still* have things in storage from my old life in Maryland: furniture, business files, and more than a hundred brown cartons, which, believe it or not, are listed on the inventory list simply as "box." But I wasn't there for that move either. Well, it's hard to be in two places at once; I'd been off at a magazine shoot. You know what it's like. How about that annual business treat (trip, sorry) you had to make to Maui, which coincided with clearing your mom's house?

Unavoidable, right? I understand your situation, but this absence may also explain your sister-in-law's mysterious frostiness and why the Queen Anne dining room table and eight chairs *promised to you* now have pride of place in *her* home. Just a thought.

In cosmic law it's not *possession* that carries nine-tenths persuasion; it's *attendance*, especially when it means showing up for your own life. Meanwhile, my New York apartment's filled with strange men eating pizza, cramming chattels into boxes, scribbling illegible words on the sides, taping them shut, and shuffling them down the elevator and into a truck illegally parked on the street.

A nonchalance hangs heavy in the air which only increases my agitation. Out of the corner of my eye I notice my assistant, midway through this bedlam, beginning to make lists of my belongings. Only now? Wasn't she also in charge of the Maryland move? Hmmm...

In an instant, I go from 0 to 100 rpms. I have become my own Cassandra; I suddenly can "see" the future and it ain't pretty. *What are in those boxes?* I want to scream. I have become She, the Dark Goddess—She Who Must Be Obeyed, She Who Pays the Bills! She the Destroyer of Worlds. I'm about to blow a no-man-ever-fathomed furor that will gather in strength across an angry sea and unleash and unfurl absolutely...nothing. That's because Miss Simpering Simple Abundance doesn't scream, doesn't shout, doesn't raise her holy "you'd better be shaking and quaking" temper. Instead she starts grinding her teeth, holding her breath until a sharp stabbing pain in the left side forces her to exhale, take a sip of water, say a prayer. (How interesting! Now I know why I hold my breath when I recall this memory. Now I know why I tried for so long *not* to recall it. Now you know why this is no way to live, no matter who you are.)

The foyer, my beautiful vestibule which once represented the expansiveness of my fabulous life, starts closing in on me like a trash compacter. The woman reflected in the Art Deco mirror is red and sweating, pacing like a caged animal looking for escape. There are hours of packing to be done and the apartment has to be vacated that night. I walk out. I can't be there. Then or now. I am supposed to be the "living embodiment" of *simple abundance*. Instead, I am consumed with the shame of losing this apartment because I haven't been a skillful stewardess of my good fortune. I have done me and mine a tremendous disservice. I walk out of the apartment. I leave Dolores Del Rio. I leave the front door ajar. I leave the foyer filled to the ceiling with brown boxes.

As I write, two years later, I still don't know where many of my things are because half the brown cardboard boxes were stored under my personal assistant's name, not mine. After all, she was the one dealing with the packers. Is it true that the things we discard tell us more about ourselves than what we hold on to? What kind of a woman leaves the tangible symbols of her hard-earned success —her beautiful possessions, her exquisite things— in the care of strangers?

A dead woman? Or a woman who's dead inside?

Excuse me, is this where the estate sale's taking place?

WAKING THE DEAD

> *Life is one long struggle to disinter oneself, to keep one's head above the accumulations, the ever deepening layers of objects and obligations which attempt to cover one over, steadily, almost irresistibly, like falling snow.*
>
> —Rose Macaulay

During the late 19th century a particular fear seized upon the psyche of English middle-class Victorians: being buried alive. This morbid concern grew out of the unreliability of the medical profession, which on occasion pronounced dead a patient who was merely unconscious. As you can imagine, when the dearly departed revived during funeral services, it caused a quite a commotion, not to mention a hue and cry for burial reform. The book *Premature Burial and How It May Be Prevented* was a sensation in 1896; it prompted a growth industry in the prevention of premature burial. At the time, people died largely at home and made their last journey to the cemetery from their own front steps, which also gave rise to the custom of families only using the front door for weddings and funerals. "Waiting mortuaries," the forerunners of funeral homes, were established so that the deceased of wealthy families could be watched around the clock by an attendant looking for any signs of life before interment. Organizations such as Society for the Prevention of Premature Encofferment, Burial and Cremation were created and products such as the Bateson Revival Device (a bell in the coffin connected to a cord placed in the deceased's hand) promoted "peace of mind amongst the bereaved in all stations of life," making its inventor, George Bateson, a very rich man.

A similar situation exists today in another unregulated funereal practice—the selling of space, not underground but above it, to store personal effects. Like the Bateson Revival Device, storage is sold with the promise of providing serenity in cubic square feet. We come into this world without anything, but we damn sure don't want to depart that way! We want our toys and treasures to come with us. Like Egyptian kings and queens we front-load eternity before the event. The original concept of storage was the cedar-lined closet used to store seasonal clothing and linens—summer and winter. The idea expanded to cedar-lined chests (to keep away moths) when immigrants took their meager personal effects across the sea to begin a new life in America or loaded a few precious possessions in trunks on prairie schooners. It wasn't until the '70s, when the baby boomers' grandparents began moving into residential nursing homes, that storage became a premium business. Your mom was having none of Nana's white and gold faux French provincial furniture "suites" anywhere in her New England Cape, so space had to be found. Nonetheless, in the architectural evolution from 19th-century Conestoga wagon to 21st-century loft conversion, lack of storage has become the Space Age's biggest problem.

"... the pyramids were built for pharaohs on the happy theory that they could take their stuff with them. Versailles was built for kings on the theory that they should live surrounded by the finest stuff," Texas writer Molly Ivins points out. "The Mall of America is built on the premise that we should all be able to afford this stuff. It may be a shallow culture, but it's by-God democratic. Sneer if you dare; this is something new in world history."

How many women's personal effects—belongings of both the living dead and the very dead—are now shrink-wrapped cubes stored in a warehouse somewhere in the South Bronx or Syracuse? What about the cryptogenic cargo holds in Seattle or St. Louis?

Eerie.

MEMORY SLIPS

Inside your home, you keep mementos of your past that help or hinder your movement into the future.

—Kathryn L. Robyn

The enormity of the human drama and sorrow being replayed on the nightly news rarely registers as houses are ripped asunder by earthquakes, tornadoes, hurricanes. Survivors stand near the wreckage of their lives and say with gratitude and disbelief: "Thank God, no one was killed. It was only things we lost." Then the news crew moves on to the next disaster and isn't there to bear witness to the shattering moment when the survivors realize that these things weren't knickknacks but symbols. Irreplaceable. Precious. To anyone else, it might look like shards of salt and pepper shakers from the Grand Canyon being swept into the garbage. But to a couple who first met at the Grand Canyon, recently celebrated their 45th wedding anniversary there, and lovingly displayed them on their sideboard, these were sacred memory vessels. Cherished objects can reveal intimate and illuminating insights into our personalities. Surrounding ourselves with objects that speak to our souls brings us genuine moments of pleasure. Still, a lot of us are numb to some objects that surround— dust gathering from past marriages and previous incarnations that have little connection to our present lives. Is your space filled with the excess baggage of old relationships— parents, siblings, roommates, lovers or spouses, children who have moved out, or of a self that you parted with long ago? Are there furnishings that may be stylish but don't reflect you anymore? Who is this woman who lives here? Are these things *you*? If they're not, what are they doing in your most intimate, personal spaces? What are they doing in *your* house?

THE HAUNTING

Does one ever see any ghost that is not oneself?
　　　　　　　　　　　　　　—Marjorie Bowen

*P*erhaps it's because women have such a difficult time letting go that we adore ghost stories. Bring up the topic of ghosts at any dinner party and most of the female guests will be able to contribute an anecdote of a sighting or a haunting, usually set in old houses.

But "objects have ghostly emanations, too, that attach themselves to their solidity," the writer Dominique Browning tells us in her marvelous book *Around the House and In the Garden*. "Things with drawers—chests, armoires, night tables, trunks—seem to be the most populated pieces of furniture."

I don't know about you, but I've never been as haunted by other people's ghosts as much as I have been by my own, especially when I open my unconscious catchalls. What stuff do *you* have squirreled away in the scary space euphemistically known as *"storage"*?

If you're like me, they're symbols of all sorts, from the sublime to the ridiculous—touchstones that provoke every emotion known to woman: letters, photographs, bank statements, lone earrings, locks of hair, one baby shoe, assorted baby teeth, menus, ticket stubs, orphaned keys, a fossilized rubber pacifier, collars of long-dead cats. In the bedroom closet, more clothes you don't wear than ones you do: clothes that make you feel uncomfortable, fat, silly, or sad. The linen closet has mismatched, threadbare rags; you don't know what's in the hall closet because you dare not open it without a hard hat.

A vibrational energy surrounds and attaches itself to every object in our homes, transforming them into palpable memories, both good and bad. Often when we feel depressed but can't identify the source of our distress, it's because we're looking for something we've hidden too well. "A person speaks not only with the voice but with those objects she chooses to surround herself," Jacqueline Winspear reminds us in her detective novel *Birds of a Feather.* "That photographs tell a story is well accepted, but the way furniture is positioned in a room tells something about its occupant; the contents of a larder reveal desire and restraint, as most surely does the level of liquid in the decanter." They all become ghostly receptacles for our "every thought, feeling, inspiration, reflection and wish."

What's ailing us is what lies just beneath the psychic surface of our lives. The things stuffed in the back of your closet, the kitchen junk drawer, attic, and basement—the past—are crying out to be buried, once and for all, or given another incarnation with someone new. Start thinking of storage as synonymous with sorrow and you'll find a new resolve to get rid of things.

"I have tried to give away some of the things in my house that have ghosts; I think they would be better off somewhere else, and I want to be rid of certain memories," Dominique Browning confesses. "The armoire that was part of a marriage, the carpet that was part of a love affair, the photograph that was part of hope, the bedcovers that were part of too many sleepless nights. Begone."

DO TRY THIS AT HOME:
GETTING OUT OF HARM'S WAY

> *There can be no harm*
> *In just remembering—that is all.*

—Katherine Mansfield

"I wear the key of memory, and can open every door in the house of my life," the Victorian writer Amelia Barr observed in 1913. When you turn the key of memory, what makes the hairs on the back of your neck stand up when you go back to certain rooms or different houses of your life? What makes your breathing go shallow? What image triggers a case of hives? What piece of furniture makes you sigh when you see it? How long have you been sighing and walking past it? What closet won't you open? Sorry to seem so down this morning, but the subject of what we pack away because we can't deal with it—brown paper packages tied up with string—these, babe, are not among my favorite things. But then neither are the panic attacks that seem to increase in direct proportion to the "stuff" that keeps accumulating. "We are all more blind to what we have than to what we have not," the poet Audre Lorde tells us.

But life and love can't be hoarded. That's the lesson which has resonated in the deepest, most personal way for me since September 11. Life is given to us in only 24-hour allotments.

We know that now. But how many days, weeks, months, and years of it have been squandered or frittered away by the protocol of pretense or preoccupation with fulfilling the needs of everyone else while ignoring our own?

Working out your personal pattern of panic attacks—the triggering of the fight-or-flight impulse (and we all have them)—is an enormous step towards ransoming back lost parts of our life, now relegated to regret. As we wander through the rooms of your home, observe your physical reactions. It may not happen at the time, but a day or a dream later you may notice something. Be alert, my love. I truly believe that regret is the only wound from which our Soul does not recover, and so I want to live without regrets. I know that the most fearful panic attacks are the ones that seem to come out of nowhere, but believe me, I also know from experience with my own crippling seizures that "nowhere" is closer than you think.

For many years I could not reflect order on the outside of my life because there was no order within. Oh, everything seemed neat on the surface, but underneath my soul was wincing in pain, my drawers chockablock with despair, and my basement seething with debris. When I was married to my daughter's father—and we'd been together 20 years when it abruptly ended—we lived for a long time over a basement that was as emotionally clogged as the Love Canal was chemically toxic. There were so many unidentified boxes crammed with books, newspapers, clothes, knick-knacks, and broken whatnots that we got to the point where we didn't even bother labeling another object before it was consigned to that subterranean landfill. Now I sigh with as much compassion as remorse when I remember that sorry basement. I did not realize it at the time, nor for a long time after our marriage ended, but that dark, cold underground was a powerful physical metaphor for the chaos and confusion that engulfed me daily. It was a profound spiritual symbol bearing silent witness to the distress my family was experiencing as my husband and I tried to keep our growing estrangement not just from the world but from each other.

Psychically exhausted and overwhelmed by the emotional and physical energy of trying to hide the unsightly—my suppressed emotions—in plain view, I lived reactively rather than reverently. Now whenever I feel stuck or mired in frustrating or distressing situations that I can't seem to change, I look around at the piles surrounding me, whether they are files, newspapers waiting to be read or recycled, or cookbooks waiting to be reshelved. I grab a box from the garage and go through it. Then I start sifting, sorting, throwing out, and putting away. Why? Because I've learned that piles of anything on your counters, shelves, tops of dressers, desks, and floors represent the unresolved in your life.

Look, you can't change your life in seven days. But you *can* get your life back on track to move on, clearing just one box a week. Deal with its issues. Now is the time.

For all those unmarked boxes consigned to the graveyards under your stairs, in the basement, attic, garage, ministorage, and/or the warehouse euphemistically known as Boxes-R-You don't just contain unresolved issues. They're packed with private woe of the worst kind: the unacknowledged. The hidden, undisclosed, disguised. The unexpressed. What about that mountain of boxes you put in the basement two years ago? Now you've been transferred and the mystery parcels are ready to be loaded on the moving van. Again. What could be in there that's so valuable? Maybe a little suppressed anger? Perhaps you not only bring home most of the bacon, but you're expected to pack the damn frying pan too? Which is exactly why you didn't unpack it *last time*. Time for a few more regularly scheduled fits of pique. "Many of our problems with anger occur when we choose between having a relationship and having a self," Harriet Lerner tells us in *The Dance of Anger*. This could be the move where you get to keep both. Pour a couple of glasses of wine, open up a box, and ask for help.

NESTING INSTINCTS:
WHAT LIES BENEATH

Moving on is about accepting what happened, not absolving it.... You will mourn. Moan and groan and grieve. You are supposed to cry about these things.

—Kathryn L. Robyn

So today seems about as good as any other to start making the connection between what we stow away and what we stew over. They're probably in the same box. One's the issue, the other's the artifacts. Proof positive, for example, that you were once upon a time married to the completely wrong man for you. But now you're happily married to your high school sweetheart (thanks to attending your 40th reunion), so by all means keep the Wizards yearbook 1974; but get rid of anything else that has to do with your previous marital incarnations, except legal papers. And no, if you have divorced her father, your daughter is not likely to want to wear your wedding dress. Sell it and buy a vintage bottle of Champagne to celebrate all the good fortune you're finally open to receive.

The sorry truth is that the longer it takes us to acknowledge whatever fear, sorrow, slights, grief, anger, abuse, neglect, contempt, betrayal, deceit, projections, errors of judgment, lack of experience, bad timing, bitter failures, rejections, bungled efforts, whims of fate, and just lousy luck we think we've packed away, all we manage to do, to paraphrase Shakespeare in describing the repetitive cycle of resentment and resignation, is "increase store with loss, increase loss with store."

Still, you can't resolve a problem or a situation that you won't admit is happening, has happened once upon a time, or you expect to happen next week. Our thoughts are like iron-mesh strapping tape. When we secretly nurse a memory with highly charged emotion, whether it's fear, sorrow, or anger, we open ourselves psychically and start inviting in all manner of misery.

Recently I met a German woman who had been married

to an Englishman and had lived in England for 20 years, when he died suddenly. By the time she attended one of my workshops about six months later, she said her grief was compounded by her fear of being deported. This had happened to her when she was a little girl, shortly after Britain declared war on Germany, and the memory of it was still very real. When she married and settled in Devon, decades later, she became a legal British resident. Still, right after her husband died she started filling her garage with empty boxes from the market. Why? Was she moving? No. She said she was afraid she'd be deported again and wanted to be ready! *Empty boxes waiting to be filled with 50 years of fear!* Those boxes were *not empty,* I told her firmly but lovingly; they were filled with her dread! I made her promise to go right home and get rid of every box. I told her she was using those boxes like magnets to attract the very thing she feared the most. When I came home after that workshop, I immediately began searching out boxes waiting to be emptied. These days I like to follow my own advice. Life's too short to stockpile heartache and too precious to be squandered piecemeal. This month I want us to get rid of as many boxes from our houses and lives as we can. Although I can't prove this beyond a shadow of a doubt, I believe with soulful certainty that there is a direct correlation between the amount of discontent, discomfort, and pain you are experiencing in your life right now and the amount of unwanted but not discarded possessions—or emotional attachments—we're holding onto and storing.

HEART REFLECTIONS:
THE BELOVED BIDS GOOD-BYE TO ALL THAT

*I*nspirer of Sublime Order, Divine Designer, who balanced the chaos of Darkness with the invocation of Light, help this woman, my dearly beloved Reader, to ransom back her home from clutter and her life from confusion. She does not know where or how to begin. Bless her with the courage to tackle her wardrobe so that she might once more find her way—and something to wear. Help her claim three hours this week to completely clean and reorganize her personal clothing, a sacred hour each for restoration of mind, body, and Soul. Remind her to come prepared with the determination to sort, sift, and say farewell, so bring to her attention the need for extra-large trash bags. Show her how to take everything out of the closet and do as you commanded—sort the space out into two distinct piles—the immediately wearable and the torn. If they're irrevocably worn out, stained, or zipperless, distract her by filling her with your Holy Spirit and toss it for her when she's not looking. (If she tries to retrieve it, remind her firmly that if this item was that important she would have had it repaired years ago.)

Encourage her to continue by asking each item of clothing the four holy questions. When were you last used or worn? Did I feel comfortable in you? When and how could you be used or worn in the future? If I were moving instead of cleaning, would I take you with me?

Now endow her with confidence to let go of the past. To realize that it's not just dresses, skirts, and pants hanging in her closet but the manifestation of memories. Forgive her and help her forgive herself her costly mistakes, comfort her with the reassurance that she does not have to entomb her regrets. Reason with her reluctance, reassure her remorse, convince her that what is really so hard to abandon are not the clothes but the pent-up emotion, frustration, disappointments, sorrow, and anger that are attached to those sorry clothes— feelings which have never been expressed or addressed in the past.

Bless her with the courage to bid adieu to what begs to be abandoned by severing the emotional threads that bind her to her shrouds of sorrow. Whether the fibers are silk, wool, or gossamer, haute couture or prêt-à-porter, help your Beloved make an unconditional commitment to her future happiness by rightfully blessing the persons or situations connected with each outfit, wishing them well, and giving them away with her blessings. Let the Spirit move her to create a Divine Void in her closet that Grace might overflow with delight in the clothes she keeps and wears.

Wipe from her brow all care and evidence of woe. Smooth her eyelids with the dust of enchantment. May her smile gladden her own heart as she so lavishly blesses others. Reveal to her all her feminine glory, and let love's passion be once again comely on her cheeks. Cinch high her waist with style and charm; reframe her wardrobe with elegance and wit. Fashion for your Beloved embroidered cloths of strength, honor, and refinement that her vision may bring praise upon all Creation. Lead her to secret designer sales. Encourage her to wear a hat with a veil and paint both her nails and the town red. Bare her décolletage so that her endowments of grace and glamour dazzle and show her how to walk in high heels.

Make merry your Beloved. Let her become her own astonishment. Grant our prayer, Weaver of Wonder, Mantle of Mercy, and let this gorgeous woman bask in her own beauty and blush according to the extravagance of Heaven's beaming, unbounded blessings.

Be it done, with all praise and honor according to Thee and joyfully accepted with thanksgiving by She.

CHAPTER FIVE

AWAKENING TO AWE

ON WOMEN AND INTIMATE PLACES

A woman's environment will speak for her life,
whether she likes it or not.

—Elsie de Wolfe

*I*t's been said that people in a crisis always fall back on what they know best: thieves to thieving, bigamists to tying another knot, gamblers to Lady Luck. My Irish Nana—a nine-day novena to St. Jude. What's your personal rescue remedy? For me, it's my bed. "There is hardly anyone in the civilized world," J. E. Buckrose confessed in 1923, "particularly those who do just a little more every day than they really have strength to perform—who has not at some time regarded bed as a refuge."

Just this morning I was thinking the same thing and told my bed so. "See you soon, sweetie" said I, patting her plump rump of a duvet appreciatively. "But not soon enough."

Every room in your house tells a story, but the most personal narratives are the whispers coming from your bedroom. What's more, a woman's bedroom is a tattletale that has no problem gossiping about her past, present, dreams for the future, or lack of them. Household confidentiality agreements? Hooey! Forget the snitch and just get me a snapshot of a woman's unmade bed; it discloses more than any tabloid snoop could ever hope to discover in your trash: your passions, peeves, pleasures, poses, and perjuries. More to the point, babe, your bed rumples reveal your self-perceptions and self-deceptions—what you secretly believe about yourself and what you think you're brilliantly disguising beneath the dust ruffle (but obviously are not).

For longer than I can bear to remember, I shared a bedroom that was small, dark, overcrowded, messy, and dreary; a hodgepodge of unarticulated disquiet between two very nice people who never really should have married in the first place. We'd been together for two years; because we were friends and genuinely enjoyed each other's company, we were probably hopeful that the power of positive thinking could replace passion. And, of course, we were in our thirties; it was getting time to settle down now. Still, I was 20 minutes late for our wedding, which took place in the living room of friends.

I was completely dressed but I was dawdling in the upstairs bedroom. On examination, it might have been my

Authentic Self tugging on my heart's sleeve trying to get my attention before I was hurried along to say "I do." No time for second thoughts! I was marrying a really lovely man, which now I know is very different from marrying a man I really loved.

We were married for three years when we were blessed with a Divine Child, a little girl with whom we immediately became besotted. There's a photo of her new daddy holding Katie within a few hours of her birth, and it's adorable.

Over the next few years, as she grew in grace and beauty before our eyes, we grew lacking in each other's, and like many other married couples with a young family we desperately wanted to do the "right thing" for her, which ended up being a highly charged emotional euphemism for duplicating our parents' marriages by sticking together and sticking it out. Ironically, we never discussed what the "right thing" was except for practical things like school, inoculations, sleepovers, and summer camp options. We never discussed anything personal; unconsciously we were both afraid that any conversation might detour into the dangerous territory of our mutual disappointments. Safer to stay busy and keep silent. Perhaps I finally found my voice on the page as a writer because I all but rendered myself mute in my marriage.

Do you know a film from 1970 called *Lovers and Other Strangers*? It was a genuinely funny movie about marriage through the eyes of a young couple and both sets of in-laws. My favorite scene is when the son tries to explain to his old-fashioned Italian father why he and his wife are getting a divorce after only a couple of years of being married. "You've got to understand, we feel there must be something more." His father just looks at him and fires back, "We all feel there's something more."

"But then, why don't you leave Mom and go out and get it, Dad?"

"Because there isn't something more!" the father roars back. And all of us know what both father and son were trying to say.

SETTLING DOWN

The real killer was when you married the wrong person but had the right children.

—Ann Beattie

*T*he mere thought is uncomfortable, but instructive. The earliest mattresses were made of muslin and hay, which is how the catchphrase "making hay" traced man's journey from the barn to the bed for his sexual romps.

During the Middle Ages, a brilliant French woman thought there had to be a better way, especially if one was trying to lure royalty to linger in her bed, so *"Madame du Quaquaqu"* experimented with stuffing her mattresses with the soft downy feathers of ducks and geese. *Vive la différence!* Soon feather beds and plump pillows became a woman's prize possessions and counted for much in a new bride's dowry. By the 1600s the expression *settling down* came to be associated with marriage, which seems a bit strange when you realize that the original implications of *settle* meant not simply to draw to a close or reach a conclusion but to conquer, appropriate property, and vanquish the enemy.

Aye, it's all *settled* now. Well, actually, up until the not so distant past, all a woman's possessions were part of a prenuptial agreement between the suitor and the bride's family and, upon completing their vows, became the chattels or belongings of her husband.

As the dancer Isadora Duncan (1877-1927), who had more proposals of marriage than she could remember, put it: "Any intelligent woman who reads the marriage contract, and then goes into it, deserves all the consequences."

Actually the word *settle* tells different tales. For we can settle *up*, settle *on,* settle *down,* and settl*e for.* I don't know about you, but at some point in my life, I've done all four. We all do: the dead-end jobs; a diagnosis that predicts you won't get well; a hurtful silence or unconscious slight; a missed anniversary; or even something as mundane as the hideous mustard-color dining room walls inherited from the previous owners three years ago. When I started writing *Simple Abundance* I'd been married for 13 years and I thought we were, well, if not happy, at least settled—mutually satisfied with the long-standing domestic arrangements.

But the truth is that our marriages are only as emotionally healthy, happy, holy, and content as we are. And neither of us was any of those things, which is why I started searching every day for something to be grateful for; the miracle of

Simple Abundance is that there is not one sad, bitter, or discordant word in that book. I pick it up today in wonderment because I know by the time I'd finished it, for the last five years of our marriage, we had evolved into two very frustrated, angry, and confused people, worn away by years of benign neglect, unarticulated assumptions, unexpressed expectations, unacknowledged disappointments; the loneliness of living with someone who is no more interested in your day than you are in his, the tedium of so much familiarity obscuring any notion of whom you're living with. Throughout our marriage my husband never desired to read my writing; so when *Simple Abundance* became a best seller, he did not know what all the fuss was about. We had grown into "the intimacy of estrangement that exists between married couples who have nothing left in common but their incompatibility," as Nadine Gordimer so chillingly describes the wasteland of the heart. Our bedroom, taking pity on us, could no longer conceal our sorrow.

THE WAY IT WAS

> *I don't think marriages break up because of what you do to each other. They break up because of what you must become in order to stay in them.*
>
> —Carol Matthau

We believe that there are only two kinds of marriages—good and bad. But really there are three: the good, bad, and the indifferent, also known as the long-standing domestic arrangement. Unfortunately, there are plenty of women who feel uncomfortable admitting to the world what they will confide in private: that their own once-upon-a-time orange-blossom dreams of wedded bliss somehow became a downward spiral of surviving—making it through the day, the week, the year, a life. Even more of us *won't* admit it, especially to ourselves. Instead, we let the bedroom go to wrack and ruin.

"... the death of a relationship seems to creep up quietly, achingly; it makes its slow, sour presence felt in strange and subtle moments. The things you think you're fighting about—sex, money, work, children—those are never really the main event," confides Dominique Browning in her exquisite book, *Around the House and In the Garden: A Memoir of Heartbreak, Healing and Home Improvement.* "They're the skewed translation of deeper problems, curled up in the dark belly of love; problems with fear, or grief, problems with scar tissue that may long ago have knit itself over too thickly."

If it's true that sometimes we marry for the wrong reasons, we convince ourselves to stay for even worse ones. I know I sailed into these turbulent waters before in my book *Something More* written in 1998, the year after my divorce, when I was trying to come to grips with the shame I felt about my marriage ending. But eight years later, my sails have been repaired, my heart has healed, and I have no choice but to finish what I started then. You see, I'm ready to move on and the only way I can do that is to make peace with my past. If I thought that my experience was singular,

I wouldn't invite you along; but moving past misery is part of our struggle to let go, and it's so much easier when a friend cheers you on, which is what I want to do for you.

"Pain is a spiritual wake-up call showing you that there are oceans you have not yet explored," Debbie Ford reassures us in her comforting and inspiring book *Spiritual Divorce*. "Divorce is a transformational time, and you can choose to use it as the fuel for creating an extraordinary life. The moment you have the life you've dreamed of you will thank God for your divorce experience, no matter how difficult the circumstances. You will naturally honor your ex-partner and support those around you in accepting your divorce. You will choose to keep your heart soft at times when you would have hardened it. Falling into the softness of your heart means slowing down, dropping your expectations and looking and living in the moment. When we are quiet enough, we reconnect with our inner knowing that life is progressing as it should"—especially if life has just taken a detour that you never intended nor could have imagined.

Debbie Ford's wise book on how to survive the devastation that comes when a marriage ceases and how to transform it into a bountiful blessing is a gift of grace. But when I first tried to read it, I resisted the book midway. In *Spiritual Divorce,* the author explores the Divine laws of acceptance, surrender, guidance, responsibility, choice, forgiveness, and creation, which all have to be set in motion if we are to rebuild our lives after divorce. Guess where I gave up? "Why should I be forgiving? Why should I give my ex-husband the gift of my loving energy?" she asks. Good questions, I'll get back to you, I said as I closed her book and put it back on the shelf. It took me years to be able to answer those questions, to discover that, as the Christian theologian Charles C. West observes, "We turn to God for help when our foundations are shaking, only to learn that it is God who is shaking them."

However, over those years as I watched Kate and her father develop a wonderful, loving relationship and saw how he helped and supported her in ways that I couldn't, forgiving my former husband seemed instinctive, especially as I had been reunited with the love of my life. Indeed, if there hadn't been our divorce, I wouldn't be so happily married today. If we hadn't been married, I would not have brought my gorgeous daughter into the world; nor would I have had the deep, personal need to write *Simple Abundance* if we hadn't been unhappily married. But it takes so much longer to forgive ourselves or our bête noire. As I've shared, even if we've staked our claim to the promised land, a lot of us have started things that need to be completely finished before we'll be allowed to start building our House of Belonging.

Always remember, it's one thing for us to understand something intellectually, like forgiveness; it's quite another for spiritual truth to register emotionally. And until it does, it's repeat and return. Return and repeat. The lesson will keep showing up. Spirit and Life become co-conspirators, committed to our highest good, even if we're not.

Personally I don't think soul growth occurs because the

student is ready and a spiritual teacher appears. I believe it's much more the case that when the soul is genuinely ready to release pain, to let go and move on, the lesson kicks in. "Grace fills empty spaces, but it can only enter where there is a void to receive it," the French mystic Simone Weil tells us, "and it is grace itself which makes this void."

OUT GO THE LIGHTS

If it's true that sometimes we marry for the wrong reasons, we convince ourselves to stay in long-standing domestic arrangements for even worse ones.

—Sarah Ban Breathnach

Of course, we stay for the children, even though the children are grown now and have children of their own. By then, we're staying out of habit. We stay because we know the address. We stay because we're house proud and deservedly so; we love our beautiful home, our joint possessions; we've worked hard for our tangible symbols that life is good. We stay because we know that when you leave, you leave the good behind as well as the bad—the cat curling around your legs as you make tea on a summer's morning, the back door open to a gorgeous breeze, and the sunlight streaming on the pretty new linoleum kitchen floor that looks like real tile. We stay because when we unwrap the Christmas ornaments, each carefully preserved happy memory pleads a halt in the heart's misgivings: "Please, don't forget me, don't leave me behind; here's the one that was the topper for the cake celebrating his law school graduation and her christening; remember how hard you looked for one; finally, you made it by hot gluing a tiny plastic baby into a funny figurine of a goofy guy wearing a cap and gown; everyone thought it was so cute and that we were so happy. And, we were, then. Remember?"

If you're a woman of a certain age (over 50), we convince ourselves to stay because we're terrified of ending up alone, pensionless, living in a one-room, cold-water flat over the sad cafe next to the railroad tracks, where you sling hash, and the only time the bed ever shakes is when the mail train to Pittsburgh passes through at 4:05 a.m. We stay because we think we can't afford to leave and won't calculate the psychic cost of remaining; our husbands always handled the money. We stay because we put loyalty to others above loyalty to our own truth. We stay because we don't even know what our own truth is, or, like I was, we're too scared at this stage to find out. We stay until we can't pretend anymore. We stay until our hands and hearts are forced. We stay, ladies, until time is called.

Look, let's be fair: if we stayed perhaps longer than we really wanted to (or we're still there), don't you think it's because we're genuinely good and decent people? I do. Good and decent people don't get married with the intention of getting a divorce, and after you've had children, the very thought of blighting their lives makes you tremble with anticipatory grief and remorse. So you sigh some more, my sweetie, sigh some more; listen to Lonestar with another glass of wine, take longer to clean the kitchen. Let the house go quiet. Out go the lights. Ache goes the heart.

The way you look standing there alone. The way this felt. Baby, when I look at you, the only thing I can see is me. The two of us, toots. Out, out, out goes the spark.

"The best marriages, like the best lives, were both happy and unhappy," Anne Morrow Lindbergh wrote in her novel *Dearly Beloved,* published in 1962. "There was even a kind of necessary tension, a certain tautness between the partners that gave the marriage strength, like the tautness of a full sail. You went forward on it."

Many years later Anne Morrow Lindbergh spoke about the worst days of her marriage, during their mutual hours of dread following her husband's delivery of his infamous Des Moines speech of September 1941, when he blundered badly by adding the issue of race to his already controversial anti-war platform. Afterward, Charles Lindbergh was widely reviled as an anti-Semitic racist and pro-Nazi sympathizer. She describes herself as being "horrified" at what he had done and admitted they had a terrible argument over it. However, when asked why she hadn't divorced Lindbergh for his racist views, she responded, "You know, when someone you've been with for years and that you love and you know does something that seems to you a total aberration, you don't walk out the door. You say, why did he do it.... And I think he did it because of a kind of blindness.... I pitied him. I pitied him. I mean, it was so awful to see this happen to him. I had a great belief in him, a great belief, and that was some of the pain."

What is so compelling about Anne Morrow Lindbergh is

that she loved her husband completely and with an uncommon intensity throughout their long marriage. They were soul mates. His public disgrace must have crushed her. Her own family disapproved strenuously of Charles Lindbergh's political positions, and this had to hurt her deeply too. And yet she stood by him, even as the halo fell and shattered, and her image and vision of him cracked too. What an upheaval she must have experienced, as the rock-solid earth of her love and belief and understanding of him shifted into quicksand. I've heard it said that the love between long-married couples eventually mellows into a state of devotion. I've also heard it said that love between two people can be measured by how much better they understand each other than anyone else, how much they put up with, and how honest they are with each other in the little things and the Big Whoppers. Whoa. Is honesty in the marriage vows? Actually, not. It's implied. Of course, we promise to love, cherish, and honor our spouses. What about adding, "Do you promise to always tell me the truth and nothing but the truth through all the changes in our lives, with the exception of whether or not I look fat in an item of clothing?" (To which the proper response is always "Only more ravishing than you looked the last time you wore it, my darling.")

"How about promising not to do anything ever that will publicly humiliate me? Or at least give me a heads up"?

I'm reminded not only of our lineage of fabulous women who became First Ladies and princesses with private marital sorrows but of an acquaintance who, if they were giving awards, would surely have been singled out for "The Loveliest Girl in the Class Award," had there been one. Years later I heard she'd married her older brother's best friend; the spark that lit their romance started blazing the night he showed up at her freshman dorm to take her to dinner on her first night at the Ivy League college they both attended. They became inseparable and following her graduation, three years on the heels of his, they married and moved to Shaker Heights, where he became a successful investment banker. Children followed, as did regular Christmas letters detailing their idyllic life together, with photos showing a smiling, united all-American family.

Then I heard he'd been arrested and sent to jail for insider trading. How utterly and completely this wonderful woman's world fell in shambles around her. Not too surprising, she seldom returns to her hometown anymore. In addition to her full-time career, she's taken on extra freelance work to pay the fine he incurred as part of his sentence and to keep the children's lives as normal as possible while he serves out his prison term. Not only did her sense of safety shatter but also her idea, based on knowing him nearly all of her life, of who he was, who they were together—and who she is now.

Although no one knows what goes on between two people (and it's really nobody else's business), virtually every marriage I've ever seen close up with family or friends or at a social distance has always appeared congenial enough to get through the stuff that makes up a life. In *Dearly Beloved*, the fascinating, obscure novel, Anne Morrow Lindbergh uses a family wedding to ruminate on marriage and the need to navigate the rocky shoals as well as the good times when the wind is full at your back. Calling *Dearly Beloved* "reflections in a fictional frame," she discloses more truths in this book about her own marriage than in any of her memoirs. This is how the mother of the bride describes her own settling down:

After all, hadn't her marriage been happy? Of course, of course it had. Deborah was sure of that. A marvelously happy marriage—a wonderful husband, beautiful children, lovely home. Everyone said so. She was the perfect wife. Everyone said that, too. Even John. She seemed to satisfy him. Wasn't that enough? What else could she want? ... What was real life anyway? Driving children to school, housework, picking up groceries, shopping, telephoning, helping with homework, passing sherry to guests before dinner; wasn't that real? No, it wasn't, Deborah decided, just scrips and scraps of other people's lives, like her bureau drawer, like her rag-bag mind—not her life at all. Someday she would break through to her own life, Deborah resolved. Now that Sally was married, she would try. Stop running around; stop wasting time; stop being the perfect mother, the perfect wife. Then she would find her own life. Where? Not here, not now. Just around the corner, out of reach.

So we schedule a potluck dinner party for the weekend and a teacher conference for Toby's reading difficulty. If you can visit your mother (who has Alzheimer's) on your way home from work, I can take Jenny to the nutritionist who specializes in eating disorders. As I said, we stay because we're good and decent people who love our families and each other, even if it's not the way we need to be loved now. We even stay in congenial, sexless marriages, especially if our family life is active, robust, and good-humored; it helps if we have a favorite couple who are close friends, with kids our kids like, and with whom we create treasured traditions—beach weekends, autumn football junkets, and holiday dinners. "You wanted to be loved in the midst of life, past your prime, paunch and grey and tired, even discouraged and cross—in all your imperfections," Anne Morrow Lindbergh confides, surely for all of us. "You wanted to be forgiven your weakness, to be loved, in spite of them, for better or for worse. That *was,* when you came down to it, what you wanted; to be loved 'for better for worse, for richer for poorer, in sickness and in health.' That was what it meant, that was what everyone wanted...."

WOMEN IN THEIR BEDS

> *Listen, my dear ones, over there across the city. Do you remember how each time you lay yourself down in a bed you wondered, if even for a moment, what you were doing there? And what about the beds you thought you'd chosen yourself? Do they now seem chosen for you? Destiny's hand patting them down, Lie here, lie here.*
>
> —Gina Berriault

Now can we stop pretending Love's got nothing to do with it? Now can we say it? There's another reason we stay in congenial but sexless marriages. We're afraid to believe in true love. Just between you and me, what do you think? Are you married to your soul mate? Well, woman, if you are, then I know what should be the first item of your Gratitude List every night. And did you tell your sweetheart today how much you love him; did you show him how much you value the gift you've both been so generously blessed with? Hint: it's in your kiss. Good, you're sorted. But what if, married or single, you don't *really* believe you'll ever find the love of your life? What if you think that if you haven't found your soul mate by 40, 50, or the third round, it's never going to happen. If that's what you think, I have a story to tell you with an improbably happy ending (the best kind, don't you think?) about lovers lost and found. But the heroine of this romance needed to start wanting her happiness as much as Spirit wanted it for her. You've got to want yours just as much. Writing of her love affair with F. Scott Fitzgerald, Hollywood columnist Sheilah Graham declared, "You can have anything you want if you want it desperately enough. You must want it with an inner exuberance that erupts through the skin and joins the energy that created the world." So, my downcast darling, this is not the day you stop believing in your happily ever after. This is the day you start.

True love exists. True love is Real.

But you know what? You're absolutely right; we don't have much chance to meet up with the love of our life if we stay where we're not supposed to be but continue to deny it on every level—spiritual, intellectual, emotional, sexual, and creative. Shortly before my marriage collapsed, I finally got up the courage to ask the man who had been my husband for 17 years, "Do you believe in soul mates?"

"No," he said matter-of-factly, the way he answered questions from clients. "I believe in accommodation." He smiled wanly and then went back to his work. I shrugged my shoulders and went to bed early. Alone. Again. A few months later, as I read something that confirmed my worst fears and broke my heart—something not meant for my eyes—I realized that sometimes genuinely nice people make terribly bad judgments close to home, and we were two of them. And that often, as Helen Rowland so wisely wrote in 1922, "When two people decide to get a divorce, it isn't a sign that they don't understand one another, but a sign that they have, at last, begun to."

THE BED YOU MAKE

> *You do not say the same thing in one room as you say*
> *in another; that is how sensitive a room is.*
>
> —Louis Kahn

There are as many bedtime stories as there are women to tell them, but the one experience all women eventually share is that the beds we make today are not always the ones we will lie down in tomorrow.

A woman reclines differently with a lover or partner than she does with her husband, as every woman who gets married shyly admits to another bride, but rarely to her bridesmaids. Married or solitary, a contented woman sprawls across the bed; a resigned woman settles in on her side for the long haul; and if she's emotionally estranged, a woman shrinks. Ironically, an unhappy woman (particularly one who has not acknowledged her plight to herself) begins to act guilty; what if her misery is discovered and then flushed out into the open? What conversation might she have to start or finish, what choice, change, or summary default will be demanded of her? Oh, no, don't worry about me. I don't need very much room. Here, let me squeeze a bit more. Suddenly every reasonable human desire, want, or need, even personal space, begins to seem excessive. See the incredible shrinking woman inch farther towards the edge of the bed, further towards the fringe of despair, nearer to the brink of extinction with each passing month. "Into how little space can a human soul be crushed?" Olive Schreiner, the 19th-century South African novelist asked. My guess? Queen-size.

Though a new divorcee and a widow might sleep alone in the bed each once shared with her husband, if betrayal's been hidden beneath the blankets, there's more likely a residue of injury and insult that remains on the other side of the bed, lingering long after he's gone. I remember my Granny not speaking kindly about Husband No. 4, which was shocking to a child of seven. She was reclining in her bed in the late afternoon wearing a long black chiffon dressing gown with ruffled collar, ropes of pearls, and waist-length Gibson Girl gray hair curled round her shoulder, very much a Colette character with a Kentucky drawl. How I loved spending time in Granny's "*bodure*." I was lying on the other side of the bed with my feet near her mound of pillows, and I had just asked her to tell me another chapter in the history of "all her husbands."

"*All* my husbands," said Granny conspiratorially. "*All my husbands?* Even the one who was hung on the hill behind Aunt Drusie's house for being a horse thief? I *forget* what number he was."

"We were up to No. 4," said I, endangering my life with my sassy mouth and missy ways. She said, "I have *nothing* to say about Husband No. 4. He's *dead.*"

Well, all of Granny's husbands were dead by this time, so to be *dead* must have really meant *something more.* "Now, hush child. No more talk about husbands. I'm going to take a nap."

When Granny said she was going to take a nap, you got off her bed real fast and out the door. "I only wish I could have k-i-l-l-e-d him *myself*," she harrumphed in a stage mutter, as her momentous mountain of Southern comfort rolled over with an equally big sigh.

It was thrilling then, and it is just as sensational now to recall. I don't know which excited me more—the fact that she'd had *four* husbands or that she wished she could have murdered one! Let's just say I have loved beds, black chiffon dressing gowns, pearls, naps, and boudoirs for as long as memory serves.

"The truth is that all of us—divorcees, widows and those

whose time has not yet come—are going to have more than one life to live," Joan Gould aptly reminds us, and that means the beds we make will change. "Sooner or later we discover that we only rent our happiness or unhappiness, we don't own it, and we'd better be prepared to move out on short notice, carrying our own suitcases at that."

L'AUTRE FEMME

The change of life is the time when you meet yourself at the crossroads and you decide whether to be honest or not before you die.

—Katharine Butler Hathaway

Women separate into two distinct groups when the topic turns to "the other woman." Whether we hear about *l'autre femme* in gossip around the water cooler, over a cup of coffee with a friend, or in the national news, we either fear or identify with her. What we really should be doing is trying to understand her hold over our emotions and imaginations. If we identify with the other woman and can argue her case, more often than not it's because we are she or have been at some point. Hold on—there are many ways to be seen as "the other woman" besides losing your way in love's guaranteed labyrinth of loss—for example an affair with a married man. Perhaps you lured away your college roommate's boyfriend 20 years ago, or you regularly flirt with a coworker's husband. Many women, including me, have had "platonic" friendships—tantalizing, emotionally satisfying dalliances with men without sexual intimacy, usually involving long lunches. We think these are sorties into "safe" neutral zones. Ha! If these liaisons are so safe, then why do we keep so hush-hush about them? This reminds me of the delicious morsel about the late, great Peggy Guggenheim, who collected art and lovers all her life and seems to have been a gal who always brought the party with her. "Hey, Peggy," a hack once asked, "how many husbands have you had?" Peggy smiled and then shot back: "My own, or other people's?"

Just as "adultery is a meanness and a stealing, a taking away from someone what should be theirs, a great selfishness, and surrounded and guarded by lies lest it should be found out," as Dame Rose Macaulay once confessed, so, too, are *les affaires platoniques,* or "French luncheons," as they are called on this side of the Atlantic. For once a woman starts sharing her mind, heart, and dreams with a man other than her husband, even if she keeps her silk knickers up, she's seriously endangering the very thing she's living as a martyr to preserve. "Love cannot survive if you just give it scraps of yourself, scraps of your time, scraps of your thoughts," the novelist Mary O'Hara reminds us. Oh, no, it cannot survive.

Look, we're all grown-ups here. We both know it takes two people to keep love alive and well in a marriage, two people to let it fail to thrive, and two to invite resignation to share room and board with them. It's only after indifference enters the picture that there's room for secrets of all kinds.

BEYOND BRICKS AND MORTAR

*There is no measuring the shock that the loss of a
house can cause.*

—Margaret Anderson

Misery loves company, so unhappily married
women seek each other out. But one friend of
mine, Maggie, tried to keep her marital problems a secret for
a long time. She, too, had a gorgeous home—a beautiful
Queen Anne revival lovingly and painstakingly restored—
in which she lived, loved, and raised six children over three
decades. She believed this was her House of Belonging. I
always enjoyed sitting at the long pine table in her gourmet
kitchen for tea and a chat. We were like the women Nora
Seton describes in *Kitchen Congregation.* "Finally, after a
pause, the conversation surges into the delta of mankind and
womankind, creeps first into the larger waterways of habit,
flows slowly between the trees of marriage, nudges softly
but persistently against the small islands of children, and
gradually fills in over the topography of daily history."

But there came a time when I started feeling vaguely
uneasy when there. Maggie was beginning renovations
again, but it seemed as if she'd just done that last year.
Smarting up the shabby bits is usually an ecstatic release for
a woman—at least it always had been for both of us. But I
became uncomfortable because I couldn't detect any real joy
in it for her this time. Something was out of balance. Finally
she admitted that her marriage of 35 years was ending

because of her husband's infidelity and that they'd been having terrible arguments. The walls had been literally eavesdropping, picking up the negative energy, and enclosing it within the living space. Now she was fixing the house up to put it on the market. In the months that followed, it was heart-wrenching for me to watch her pack up a lifetime of memories and go through the motions of moving on.

There is absolutely no way you will *ever* do that, I told myself emphatically. About this time I also got very busy with work and I made an interesting connection. I discovered that, just as mutually unhappily married women seek each other's company, married women who pretend they're happy *avoid* their friends going through a breakup because we think divorce is catching.

So it was a long time before I was able to pay a belated housewarming visit to the new house Maggie had bought with money from her divorce settlement. I remember feeling awkward as I rang the doorbell on my first visit. From the outside, the small suburban townhouse was as plain and unassuming as her former home had been grand and imposing. I couldn't believe it had come to this. Besides enduring the pain of divorce and losing a house she'd adored, was my friend now living with the discomfort of trading down?

But when she opened the door, Maggie looked ten years younger. Her glowing face and enthusiasm revealed that in the most important ways her life had been upgraded. In fact, I'd rarely seen her so serene. It seems that her former husband's seasons of infidelity had had long stretches; living with chronic pain, whether it's your back or heartbreak, is exhausting. As she gave me the grand tour of her new home, I became enthralled. Obviously she hadn't been able to keep all her furniture, but the pieces she did bring with her looked enchanting in their new setting. Her new house radiated a warm hospitality that seemed organic: it was as if the walls, windows, ceilings, fireplaces, and floors possessed human qualities.

"This house chose me," Maggie said simply. "I just can't explain it. The first time I crossed the threshold, this dear little place said, 'Welcome Home.'" As she led me through each light-filled room, the peace of her new refuge was palpable. The house felt like a loving shelter. I had not been having a good day; but here, drinking afternoon tea and basking in the benediction of a cherry tree blooming outside her living room window, I remembered what contentment felt like. When I left, I blurted out something ridiculous at the time. I asked Maggie to put me first on the list and call me if she ever wanted to sell it. We had a good laugh because she said, "There isn't a man *alive* I'd leave this house for," and sounded as if she meant it. What's more, the bijou house could only hold two people comfortably. At the time I was still married, Kate was a teenager, and we had three cats. More important, I didn't have any money of my own. I'd just turned *Simple Abundance* in to my publisher and was still getting $250 every two weeks for housekeeping money from my husband (if I asked nicely). The thought of buying my own house was preposterous.

Ah, the mystical chain of chance unfolds at its own pace and with perfect timing.

"Everyone and everything is supposed to work according to some master plan; few would have the temerity to admit that chance or mischance plays any part in the order of his or her life," wrote the Duchess of Winsdor in her memoirs, *The Heart Has Its Reasons,* explaining she never intended that her husband abdicate the throne of England for little her. "Yet I often find myself wondering whether there has been some sort of plan that controlled my life."

A year later, the phone rang. Maggie had fabulous news. She was getting married again to her soul mate, Joe, who was a widower. He'd been happily married and his dying wife had gifted him with the hope that he not remain alone after she was gone. A few years had passed and destiny got Maggie and Joe to the same church supper. Their wedding was a joyous event. I attended alone, and as I heard them pledge to each other, I thought about how much courage people needed to make marriage vows. You never think about marriage and courage at the same time when you're young, do you?

As for me, *Simple Abundance* was just hitting its stride and I was desperately trying to reconcile my private sorrows and my own mantra to my readers: *All you have is all you need. All you need is the awareness of how much you have and be grateful for it.* I got so much mail and so many requests that I needed to hire people to help me. My husband was tired of the people coming in and out of the house at all hours. I didn't blame him. The boundaries between home and work were dangerously blurred. I'd just sold another book, which helped me buy Maggie's townhouse for an office. I could move *Simple Abundance HQ* to her serene, orderly, beautiful space. So practical. All I have is all I need. Yes, Lord. I'm so grateful now to have a place of my own, to write, to think, to dream, and to create. But I couldn't deny it. Everything at home was in complete chaos. I had yet to realize that, as Mona Van Duyn tells us, "There is no disorder but the heart's."

HOME ALONE

> *In a time when nothing is forever and even tomorrow can feel uncertain, when our sense of self can be dashed in a day, by work gone wrong, or gone mechanical, by love gone awry or a careless word, there is always bed.*

—Ilse Crawford

*I*t's a strange and wondrous thing to regain not only a bed but to reign over an entire realm after sharing the bedroom for so long. Getting used to an abundance of personal space in which to stretch, spread out, and sink down is a self-indulgence you, too, can become accustomed to. But there's no need to go through a major change such as divorce to change your life for the better. What you need is to make your presence known in the marriage and in the bedroom. "Your bedroom should be the most intimate and private room in the house. If it is not, then it is a little sad," said the late, great interior designer Mark Hampton. "The kind of personal indulgence I'm talking about shouldn't even be exposed to the criticism of others. It really should be private. A result of all this delicious privacy is the freedom to gather around yourself all the trappings of personal comfort and luxury. This does not necessarily mean gold boxes or Leonardo drawings. It means wonderful linens of whatever style or era you prefer, enough pillows and quilts and blankets to make you comfortable…. The only dogma worth observing is one that is self-imposed."

Probably because I am a woman I approached my new singleness with purpose, as a decorating project, beginning with the bedroom; I could concentrate on paint swatches and fabrics while adjusting to the fact that I could now cry myself to sleep on either side of the bed.

It was all over so quickly. In an ordinary instant. A tornado rattling around the walls like a wailing woman. A total eclipse of the heart. The Truth is the only thing that ever stands between broken hearts and Wholeness. And here's my Truth: If a despair that begins as a daily disquiet between two people is ignored in private, it will grow in strength and intensity until it becomes a roar of rage that will not be denied until the anguish becomes outward, palpable expressions of your shared sorrow: alcoholism, accidents, affairs, or heart attacks. When the silence becomes deafening in a marriage and it's all over but the shouting, it's meant to be all over. So you ask Spirit for grace, guidance, clarity, and peace. If you have and hold not, you ask Spirit for help to hang on or let go. You ask for courage to move on. "It isn't for the moment you are stuck that you need courage," Anne Morrow Lindbergh comforts us, "but for the long uphill climb back to sanity and faith and security." You ask your heart if you should stay or leave. If you are meant to stay, you ask for the gift of a willing heart, patience, and forgiveness. If you are meant to leave, you will be shown the path. You ask your Soul to be shown how to leave with honor, honesty, integrity, and Love.

I held the keys to my little townhouse, the dear little place now full of brown boxes waiting to be organized into an office. The empty space that chose me, waiting for me to embrace the gift of sudden change, the void that only Grace could fill.

DO TRY THIS AT HOME:
BED FOR BEGINNERS

For me the bedroom is the most important room of the house. It should be exactly what you are...If I describe my bedroom, I describe myself.

—Madame Irith Landeau

Just as the words "night" and "sleep" are not synonymous, neither are "bedroom" and "boudoir." By the way, what are you doing in your bedroom? Don't tell me you're sleeping because I won't believe you. For if you've managed this miracle without opiates, then you certainly don't need my advice. So let's think of other reasons for having a bedroom. Repose, rest, relaxation, reading, and, of course, romance?

I fear that a woman's bedroom has not become the refuge for which it was originally intended. How about the communal Home Ec center—the place we end up ironing, mending clothes, bill paying, exercising, catching up on the news, and passing through on our way to crawling over the covers and plopping down, dead as a stoat, until the alarm goes off sounding like a starting pistol for the next 24-hour sprint. Sound too close for comfort?

Good. Now we're getting somewhere.

Believe it or not, what you need isn't a bedroom, it's a boudoir. A place to beat a classy retreat, where you retire instead of unravel.

The writer Judith Thurman tells us that the boudoir, a personal space quite apart from a French woman's bedroom, was literally "a room in which to sulk, for *bouder* in French means 'to sulk.' This is a wry and rather elegant way of signaling a need most women share but don't in reality admit to: the need to be invisible."

She continues our French lesson: "You can hide in any room with a good lock on the door. But the boudoir is to a spare bedroom what a peach silk peignoir is to a terry cloth bathrobe (which turned pink when you washed it with your daughter's gym uniform).... The sumptuousness of a boudoir is essential to its nature. It's a form of nourishment, or respectful self-indulgence."

Can you think of any reason a woman might want to be invisible in her own house? Well, time alone doesn't just mean taking a nap. Judith Thurman offers us some amazing boudoir suggestions: "staring at a fire, watching the rain, listening to music through a set of headphones, reading catalogs, stenciling a picture frame, fantasizing about an old flame, doing a double-acrostic while drinking an entire pot of espresso, trying to explain oneself telepathically to one's mother, writing a seductively critical letter to a famous novelist that will never get mailed, sorting one's panty hose by color, studying palmistry or ancient Greek, making an evening purse from the scraps of some old silk ties. Sulking—refusing to be cajoled or intimidated by the demands of other people or of reality—has been vastly underrated as a balm for the stresses of a woman's life."

True, not many of us have separate rooms for our boudoir, but creating one is more a state of mind than of space. If you can, how about moving out the computer, exercise equipment, or ironing table? Okay, maybe not yet, but don't give up trying! In that case, what about using a screen or long curtains to hide them from your sleeping area?

Keep your bed for the bliss of a good sleep or lovemaking; if you do, you may discover you get more of both. Use a chair, daybed, or desk for serious reading and writing, and be vigilant about banning work from your boudoir.

To decorate, you already have things that you love but don't trot out too often. How about silk scarves or crocheted shawls as table coverings? Hang a fluttery negligee or evening wrap over the edge of a closet door or on the back of a chair; prop a fancy hat angled over a mirror. Arrange tiny, clear Christmas tree lights around the outline of your headboard. Replace your practical curtains with sheers of fabrics—a double layer of tulle or chiffon becomes cascades of moonlight or streams of sunlight to dance on your floor. If you really get carried away, take a pair of inexpensive white curtains and dye them black; it's so sexy and fabulous, whether you choose to share your boudoir with someone else won't become just a rhetorical question.

Personally I think a woman should be rapturous about her bed coverings and obsessive about what lies beneath them. How do your sheets *feel* against your skin? Are they stiff, unforgiving, worn thin, or ratty? Silk sheets cost the earth, but they wash well and last for years without showing their age, keeping you warm in the winter, cool in the summer—and perhaps encouraging you to adopt Marilyn Monroe's advice to wear only Chanel No. 5 to bed. Pillows. I've rarely passed a beautiful one by, and then I've regretted it! Ruched, tasseled, tufted, silk, velvet, embroidered, trimmed, beribboned, festooned, the imagination boggles. You can move them anywhere, everywhere and be delighted with how they perk up a corner.

No, it is not possible to be too extravagant when it comes to creating your boudoir!

Always indulge in a bouquet of fresh flowers or fragrant seasonal plants; seek until you find the most gorgeous scented candle that you only use in your boudoir. (My selection right now is Miller Harris's Bois de Savage.) Take time to find a fabulous throw to toss over the end of your bed to encourage naps. Group your perfume bottles on a pretty mirror, silver, or decoupage tray. Ransom gorgeous candle holders from a thrift shop. Plant a window box even if it overlooks your own backyard. Find the prettiest *Do Not Disturb* sign and hang it on the door, then supplement it with an inside chain lock. If you have the space, trade in dinky little bedside tables for larger ones.

And finally, have the following signage stenciled and framed to hang over your bed, just like mine:

TRUE PASSION IS INTOXICATING AND INVIGORATING,
SOOTHING AND SENSUOUS, MAGICAL AND MYSTICAL.
I JUST THOUGHT YOU SHOULD KNOW WHAT YOU'RE IN FOR!

NESTING INSTINCTS:
VANITY OF VANITIES

I don't want to be reasonable—there's plenty of time for that in the grave. What I want is adventure, innovation, foolishness and discovery.

—Mirabel Osler

And a dressing table. I want the luxury of sitting down to do my makeup at a kidney-shaped table with a billowing skirt, a beveled-glass top, and a beautiful mirror. A table by the window to see myself in natural as well as incandescent light. "The lure of the dressing table is its promise of transformation. We come to it nose shiny and hair awry, a fright, and rise up powdered sleek, a sight for sore eyes," writer Cynthia Zarin reminds us. "In addition to its transforming powers, the dressing table is a place of rapprochement. We fall out constantly with our own faces. We despise our noses, despair over our chins. But with blushes and shadows, we make up."

Early influences affect us more than we realize. When you were young what woman seemed to be the most glamorous—an older sister, an aunt, an actress? Did your mother remind you to wash your neck and behind your ears? Laugh with me here, sweetie, because we've spent too much of our lives crying and not knowing why. I wish this weren't true, but there is a link between what they used to call "personal daintiness" and our homemaking. Depending upon which side of the coin is up, it's called self-esteem or self-loathing.

"Your opinion of yourself is based to a remarkable extent on your care of your body," Margery Wilson wrote in *The Woman You Want to Be* published in 1942. "To keep up your courage, keep up your grooming. Nothing aids morale so much as a feeling of physical freshness—and nothing damages it so much as a little neglect."

Every woman deserves one place that can serve as an altar to her vanity. A sensuous space where she can keep her perfume bottles, potions, and puffs. It can start as small as a vanity case, then move to a dresser top or a top shelf on a low bookcase. Make room for a small table or even a piece of door on sawhorse legs. Go to a fabric store and find yourself the prettiest fabric in the remnant pile because you'll want reams of it to cover and drape to your heart's content. Next to an eyelash curler, a staple gun is a woman's best friend.

Not long ago my frustrated longing for a vanity took an extreme turn for the better. In a vintage shop, I found a black net petticoat from the '50s with layers of fabulous flounce. I placed it over a small table to make a bouffant skirt. Hmmmm ... it needed something more. I remembered two reversible red silk curtain panels—plaid on one side, red polka dots on the other—that I bought years ago because I loved the print. I threaded them with a black and white polka dot ribbon and tied them around the table, pinning back the corners so that both sides of the fabric showed and the petticoat peeked underneath! So saucy! Then I put a flea market mirror on top. I created this darling dressing table for my boudoir in about an hour. It's not big enough to sit down to complete my maquillage, but it's a tiny jewel of a start, which makes me smile just to see it. I know where I'm headed.

"When Sleeping Beauty wakes up, she is almost 50 years old," the poet Maxine Kumin consoles us. I would say just about old enough to appreciate the glories of a dressing table, wouldn't you?

HEART REFLECTIONS: THE BELOVED BESEECHES HEAVEN TO WRAP HER IN COMFORT AND AWAKEN HER TO AWE

Weaver of Dreams, hush the harried heart of your Beloved and hear her this eventide. As the shadows lengthen, let her sorrows disappear and fears fade. Gentle Shepherdess of Slumber, let her not be restless, wakeful, in danger or despair. Soothe her frazzled mind, and brush from her brow the cares she has courageously carried for others all day. Ransom, retrieve, and return to her the strayed or shattered and scattered parts of her soul. Restore in this night's reveries her grace and repose. Replenish energy consumed by overwork and good intentions. Infuse her with good humor and joie de vivre.

As she snuggles down in the Simple Abundance you have set apart for her—this beautiful, bountiful bed—wrap her in comfort and tuck her in safety. Bless, protect, and preserve all those she loves and keep watch over her House of Belonging. And when the darkness eases into the miracle of morning, awaken her with awe at the gift of another day in Paradise.

Be it done, with all praise and honor according to Thee, and accepted with thanksgiving by She.

CHAPTER SIX

PEEL HER A GRAPE
ON WOMEN AND THEIR KITCHENS

Whatever happens in the kitchen, never apologize.

—Julia Child

To write the truth about women in their kitchens is to write about so much more than a room, cooking, food, or recipes—and it's about as easy as peeling a grape.

"It seems to me that our three basic needs, for food and security and love, are so mixed and mingled that we cannot straightly think of one without the other," M.F.K. Fisher recalls. Mary Frances Kennedy Fisher was arguably this country's greatest food writer and knew all about the holy hungers and the celebration of Simple Abundance to be found in pleasures of food and bed: "I cannot count the good people I know who to my mind would be even better if they bent their spirits to the study of their own hungers." She knew that a woman's kitchen is the sacred space where, daily, we must seek the feminine three-in-one—the holy trinity of love, security, and food—and then share them with those who seek solace and shelter under our roof.

However, in order to meditate upon a woman's kitchen means we must prepare a meal, inviting to the welcome table not only our familiars—family, friends, lovers, children—but our prodigal outcasts as well: the forbidden, the forgotten, and the forsaken who furtively forage on the scraps of our mistakes, nibbling away at the refuse of remorse, burrowing into the compost of our guilt. If, as Oscar Wilde recommended, "revenge is a dish best served cold," so, too, is reconciliation. After the fever has subsided, the angry words are just the faintest echo, after the passage of time and the bestowing of wisdom. Cold meats and salads for our buffet, don't you think? I make the best potato salad in the world, so I've been told. It's my mother's never-fail recipe. What cold dish will you prepare?

Good then. Let us call them forth. Recollections of the celebratory feasts, sensual suppers, and scanty cupboards. Memories of when the pantry was well stocked, along with the leaner times when we learned how to cook a wolf (thank you, M.F.K. Fisher)—a talent every woman should have in her repertoire. Call to them all. Go out into the fields and on the byways. Come, sip, sup, savor, and sigh. Guests from

Christmases past, the baby shower, the birthday tea, the christening, the commencement, the promotion barbeque, Thanksgiving feasts, the wedding reception, summer picnics, autumn tailgates, the golden anniversary bash, drinks and finger food after the funeral.

Now call to mind all those meals prepared to satisfy the hungry, the hard-to-please, and the horny with their hands up your skirt as you're trying to smooth the lumps out of the gravy; you've made thousands. Don't forget the constant cravings. The crumbs in bed. The mornings of imperishable bliss and the melancholy midnight raids in front of an open refrigerator door, seeking in the cling-wrapped leftovers the tender mercies your Soul needs now.

When she turned 50, the Peruvian writer Isabel Allende realized that her biggest source of sighs—remorse *and* pleasure—were associated with food and sex. And so, repenting of her diets and "all the delicious dishes rejected out of vanity," as much as lamenting "the opportunities for making love that I let go by because of pressing tasks or puritanical virtue," she set forth with pen and spoon on a "mapless journey through the regions of sensual memory...."

Peel her a grape for sustenance. And one for you—and me too. The result of Isabel Allende's passionate pilgrimage back to her lustful culinary past became *Aphrodite: A Memoir of the Senses,* a luscious, charming, and saucy exploration of the sensual arts of food and love, especially the bewildering array of substances and practices from around the world believed to arouse passion and desire—aphrodisiacs. Here is a cookbook meant to be devoured in bed, with or without a lover. I didn't even realize I was alone as I savoured every word.

Ah, well, whether to bed or to the table, you'd be foolish not to come, woman, when you are bid. But aphrodisiacs? I can barely get the word out without memories of high school locker door whispers of tales of "Spanish fly" or ghastly concoctions of crocodile semen and powdered rhinoceros horn. Why not think about violets, chocolate, coffee, asparagus, honey, basil, peaches, or pears? They're much more pleasant. But down through the centuries, these natural wonders, too, have also been coveted and church-condemned because of their abilities to kindle romantic urgings. If that's the criteria, I'll just add a bit of Cole Porter and a chilled glass of Champagne as we shake off a tabootie or two.

Let our kitchen chimera conjure up tantalizing tidbits and tempting teasers, a plateful of *amuse-bouche,* bite-size delights to amuse the mouth; naughty, erotic, feminine fantasies of carnal pleasures; and the most powerful aphrodisiac of them all—a woman's imagination: a man who cuddles your soft, saggy middle at the sink or in the dark of the night and thinks your body's gorgeous, all curves and comfort. This same man makes you laugh—and how you both do when you wear saucy ruffled aprons, black seamed stockings, open-toe high heels to dish up his favorite dessert, bare bottom buttermilk pie. Yummy kitchen: lipstick red enamel coffeepot; the aromas of moist, dark gingerbread; succulent turkey skin torn off the breast when no one's in the kitchen but you and gobbled up in secret; melted caramel; whipped *crème;* chocolate batter, finger-sucking good; and a set of six matching pink Pyrex casserole dishes. We deserve to be spoilt and here's my list to start. What's in your Yummy kitchen?

"The kitchen is the one place in which we're all required to begin again, each day, at ground zero," the culinary historian and cookbook author Betty Fussell reminds us this morning over a delicious cup of coffee, smelling as good coffee should, like bitter chocolate. "It's the place where, if we but have eyes to see, we can see the miraculous in the ordinary—can see each day the water turn into wine, wine into vinegar, flour into bread, milk into butter, butter into cheese, loaves and fishes into food for multitudes…. memories fail, as recipes do, because what's inside the head and what's on the plate are never the same, no matter how hungry we are to bring them together."

And when we do bring them together in one room—the memories, the recipes, the faith we need to know that our holy trinity —love, food, security—is worth believing in, living for, then why should a woman's kitchen also trigger as many bittersweet contradictions, cravings, and confessionals as they do of nourishment and nurturing? Could it be the memory of mouthwatering, heart-warming, soul-satisfying lasagne and cherry cheesecake that we prepared for others— but denied ourselves? Or is it because more than any other room in a woman's house, her kitchen symbolizes the two secrets which shame her the most: her relentless pursuit of perfection and her ruthless denial of self-pleasure.

Paradise lost.

EVERYDAY EDENS

"...I can't help but sighing for lost Edens."

—Sylvia Plath

Back in the seventies, during my single/white/female days (pretending to be a grown-up in the Big City, but only as risqué as *That Girl*'s cutesy Marlo Thomas and perky Mary Tyler Moore), there suddenly came along a very scary movie—the 1975 film *The Stepford Wives,* based on Ira Levin's chilling novel about the compulsory perfection of women in a small Connecticut town. It seems that Stepford had been a haven of women's libbers during the bra-burning '60s, until all the men in town formed a secret association to replace their rebelling wives with smiley, submissive, sundress chic, domestic divas—full-time homemakers, happy to scrub floors; raise adorable, beautifully behaved children; prepare gourmet meals; and provide wild, raunchy sex. Welcome home, darling ... the perfect martini and canapés at six o'clock with a come-hither smile and a wink. (Well, what else was the kitchen table for if not your own galloping gourmand and hot pussycat romps after the kiddies were tucked away?)

I saw nothing worrying or wrong here; they were *married,* for gosh sakes. But what was sinister was the notion that just as I had reached the point where I could seriously start to play house, all that I deemed sacred—iconic images of perfect wives, mothers, and homemakers—were being so cleverly mocked, undermined, and denigrated.

Like many baby boomer women, I was thrown way off-kilter by the suddenly changing roles of women in the late '60s and '70s, catching my kitten heels on my maxi coat as I rode the up-escalator to the executive suite where I worked as a legal secretary.

This was the era of the post-war kitchen debates, and it wasn't President Richard Nixon or Soviet leader Nikita Khrushchev who had women's attention as much as the battle royal between the "Bettys" for feminine hearts, minds, and souls. Next to the stove in one corner of the kitchen was America's beloved Betty Crocker, stirring with her big wooden spoon as she taught future homemakers of tomorrow how to make cookies called "Beau Catchers and Husband Keepers." Fictional though she may have been (created by General Mills to answer baking questions sent in by women), Betty Crocker had reassuringly reminded women through four tumultuous decades of change—an economic depression in the '30s, the war years of the '40s, and the postwar boom in the '50s—that "a homemaking heart" will give you "more appeal than cosmetics" and "good things baked in the kitchen will keep romance far longer than bright lipstick." On the other side of the kitchen, by the open back door, glowered Betty Friedan, author of the manifesto *The Feminine Mystique,* which ordered women out of their aprons and into pantsuits. She claimed that women like my mother were being held under house arrest, trapped like squirrels in a cage.

"The feminine mystique has succeeded in burying millions of American women alive," Betty Friedan declared, liberating women from the "problem that has no name—which is simply the fact that American women are kept from growing to their full human capacities." She warned that this was "taking a far greater toll on the physical and mental health of our country than any known disease" and each suburban woman struggled alone. "As she made the beds, shopped for groceries, matched slipcover material, ate peanut butter sandwiches with her children, chauffeured Cub Scouts and Brownies, lay beside her husband at night—she was afraid to ask even of herself the silent question—'Is this all?'"

Well, personally, those so-called burdens sounded like blessings to me then, and they still do and rate quite a few entries in any woman's Gratitude Journal. But still, at 18, I was very confused; so was my 16-year-old sister, and so was our mother. There was something in what Betty Friedan said, and we were stumped over how to justify both impulses lurking inside ourselves. It may have been too late for many of the boomer's moms to suddenly find "meaningful work" that did not include marriage or raising a family. But there was still a chance for their daughters, even if once we arrived at the office we were serving coffee to a boss instead of a husband.

KITCHEN WARS

> *Every woman of my generation is sick of war. Fifty years of war. Wars rumored, wars beginning, wars fought, wars ending, wars paid for, wars endured.*
>
> —Josephine W. Johnson

"I've spent most of my life doing kitchen battle, feeding others and myself, torn between the desire to escape and the impulse to entrench myself further. When social revolutions hustled women out of the kitchen and into the boardroom, I seemed to be caught *in flagrante,* with a potholder in my hand. I knew that the position of women like myself was of strategic importance in the war between the sexes. But if you could stand the heat, did you have to get out of the kitchen?" asks the culinary historian and cookbook author Betty Fussell in her engaging memoir, *My Kitchen Wars.* "Yes, we were increasingly restless in our kitchens, and many of us tried to parlay our voluntary services into paid ones. But we didn't want to be liberated forcibly, any more than the hookers on Forty-second Street wanted to be liberated by flying wedges of affluent Women Against Pornography.... I had invested too much in my decades of caretaking, which despite its frustrations had meaning to me. I couldn't simply exchange one role for another, so like countless other women I took on both, doing double the work in the same amount of time." And so in order that she could both cook, write, and stay at home, Betty Fussell began writing about food.

A WRITER IN THE KITCHEN

Her life is cooked and digested.
Nothing but leftovers in Tupperware.

—Marge Piercy

Now that Mom realized that the source of her deep domestic depression and secret self-loathing was wasting all those years creating a comfortable home for her husband and four children, my mother also felt the need to find "meaningful" work outside the realm of the kitchen. She filled in a magazine coupon featuring one of her favorite authors, Faith Baldwin, who declared it was a pity that more women who were full-time homemakers didn't break into "the exciting and lucrative field of freelance writing." Soon large mysterious envelopes addressed to my mother began arriving from the Famous Writers School.

Thus, there was a period during the '60s when our family rhythm, not to mention our menus, revolved around what was going on at the kitchen table during the day when we were in school and Dad was at the office. These were Mom's writing "assignments" for the month, personally approved tutorials from one of the illustrious members of the FWS Guiding Faculty, which included Bennett Cerf, Jessamyn West, Faith Baldwin, Rod Serling, and Bruce Catton. I don't remember any of her writing assignments, but I sure do remember the writer's menus. During the week when Mom's assignment arrived, dinner was always an easy one-skillet splendor—Spanish rice, beef stroganoff, or a

"Drusilla-meal," as she called it (usually macaroni and cheese with chopped meat), the memory of which puts Hamburger Helper to shame. Mom had the preparation of these fast and fabulous one-dish dinners down to ten minutes, all the while devouring her current writing challenge. With a clarity that is heartbreaking, I can see her now: standing at the stove, stirring with her right hand, reading her assignment on a sheet held aloft in the left.

During the next couple of weeks while she'd be percolating, pondering, and procrastinating (as all writers do!), we'd eat casseroles (tuna, soup-can surprise, sweet-and-sour pork, south of the border chili) prepared early in the day, slowly baked in the late afternoon and served piping hot at 6 p.m. If Mom was really blocked, she prepared her favorite comfort meal, which became mine and is sure to be my last culinary request: soup beans, a personal time-travel transporter to her own mother's Kentucky kitchen. Soup beans are pinto beans that have simmered slowly for hours until they create their own soup. Now ladle the soup beans over mashed potatoes, serve with coleslaw, hot corn bread slathered with real butter, followed by jam cake with caramel icing. A successful completion of that month's assignment and we were all rewarded for her hard work with Sunday food, even on a Wednesday: pot roast or fried chicken, with chocolate cream pie for dessert.

All the writing assignments were graded, and failure to live up to her own impossible expectations meant soup and sandwiches for a week—or at least until the next envelope arrived. Can you imagine paying people to tell you the best you'll ever be is mediocre? My mother never published a single word, nor lived to read any of my books. She's been dead for over a decade now, and I've just remembered the last time that I visited her she made me soup beans, about two weeks before she died from complications of a fall in her, by then, tiny kitchen. I tried to make them once after she died and scalded my arm very seriously when I mishandled her pressure cooker. I never could understand how that contraption worked. I guess I've been hungry for a long, long time now.

KITCHEN CONGREGATION

> *This is not my recipe. This is a memory, retrievable only as memories are, by evocation and gesture and occasional concreteness that is not factual. And I resist making it a recipe. This is about art and love, not about technique. Some things need to be learned standing beside someone.*
>
> —Elizabeth Kamarck Minnich

M y mother shared some recipes with me, but I can't really say she taught me to cook. I don't have any memories of standing beside her at the stove, a confession which brings tears to my eyes. All I know about cooking I learned from other writers in the kitchen. The late, dearly missed Mary Cantwell taught me how to cook in the early 1970s when she wrote a cooking column for *Mademoiselle*. I mastered the mysteries of macaroni and cheese (which my teenage stepsons swoon over) and the personal sense of pride a woman feels when she knows that, if she had to, she could throw together a Christmas pudding.

Later in the 1980s, after I was first married to Kate's father, my cooking mentor and much loved writer in the kitchen was Laurie Colwin. She taught me how to make gingerbread—and that really good olive oil, sweet butter, and organic chickens were affordable luxuries, even when the wolf was at the door. Our lives were very similar—we were close in age, each had one daughter, and both of us wrote for a living. But most of all, Laurie Colwin and I were dedicated homebodies who found delight and excitement right here at home. Both of our days were structured around scribbling things down on paper, after-school activities, pot roasts, and the shared belief that good cooking is a high art—the holy trinity of love, security, and food.

Another thing we shared was an infatuation with cook-books. "No one who cooks cooks alone. Even at her most solitary, a cook in the kitchen is surrounded by generations of cooks past, the advice and menus of cooks present, the wisdom of cookbook writers," she reminds me as I thumb through my dog-eared, grease-stained collection of her cooking essays, *Home Cooking: A Writer in the Kitchen* and *More Home Cooking: A Writer Returns to the Kitchen.* And how dearly present she remains in my kitchen, though she died in her sleep, at 48, a decade ago.

I have had since my mother's death a flowered accordion file containing her recipes, which until this afternoon I've not been able to bring myself to even untie. Corn bread, seafood cocktail (only as the appetizer for holiday dinners), Mom's mouthwatering sage dressing (not stuffing!), spaghetti (not pasta!). But here is a recipe I don't believe was ever served at our table: *"Cream Mongole with Sherry, serving 5–6."* Basically it's two cans of soup—tomato and pea—with light cream, sherry, and Worcestershire sauce. Basic instinct raises doubt. But who knows? Mother has neatly typed out this recipe on a formal recipe card for a reason (maybe when she had writer's block, she thought she'd bring order to her mind and kitchen with typed recipe cards). Was this soup to impress guests? The imagination is drawing a blank. When we had "company" Mom made Clams Casino and Oysters Rockefeller. How proud I was to offer them, beaming in the praise she wouldn't accept for herself.

But I do remember her penchant for tiny newspaper scrap bundles, and they're all here—yellowed and crumbling recipes for Salmon Croquettes, Shrimp Orleans, Chicken Legs Piquant, and Pork Chops Germaine, folded into tiny squares like origami puzzles. Here, too, the 1958 Dryden Street School sixth-grade class fund-raiser cookbook, as well as a note from my granny to her "Baby" dated 1956 "while watching Ed Sullivan" and warning Mom about the dangers of aluminum. "Do *not* use aluminum foil to wrap anything in, unless it's cold biscuits."

Well, this certainly clears up the Saran Wrap mystery. Except for Thanksgiving when it lined the roasting tin to catch the bird's drippings, I rarely saw a roll of aluminum foil in our kitchen drawers. Hmmm, secretly I'd hoped she might have surprised Dad at the door one evening when the kids were otherwise amused. I guess not.

"The kitchen is about the re-creation of childhood the way you wanted it to be, keeping all that was wonderful in your own early years, while weeding out those things that caused pain. We remember the hubbub of women, the warm sweets and hovering smells, the junction of food and love, the wrapping hug of the wainscoting of counters and ovens around the walls, the inkling that one might always find a mother there," Nora Scton reminds all of us in her luminous memoir, *The Kitchen Congregation.* "The kitchen slips noiselessly into the dreams of our children before they are conscious of it, before they have children of their own, and wake up. Mothers and daughters share the kitchen with a common knowledge of women passing their lives there— at the sink, the stove, scanning the shelves of the pantry. The walls are our backsplash. Our laughter glazes the counter-tops. Here and there are the scratches that mark our moments of anguish. We cry at the sink, blotting our tears with damp dishtowels."

Nora Seton believes it's very important that we don't con-fuse kitchens with food, and I couldn't agree more. "Kitchens are about process, about the making of the meal, those hours, a quiet retreat or a din of beloved voices, the preparation of a favourite or sacred recipe, like the staging of a private play." A passion play, with mysterious final scenes.

My darling husband, Jonnie, pokes his head in the door.

It's getting late. He wants me to stop now. Join him in the kitchen. Fix his ritual gin and tonic, let him open a bottle of wine for me, and see what we can rustle up together for a bijou snackette. It's our time to reconnect or at least an opportunity to put on my ruffled pink gingham apron and give him a wink and a kiss.

"What's for dinner tonight?"

This moment is too good to be true as only moments in a woman's kitchen can be.

"How about a surprise, darling? Cream Mongole with Sherry."

KITCHEN CONFIDENTIAL

Memory is hunger.

—Ernest Hemingway

Virginia Woolf believed that very few women write truthful memoirs, and I know why. Memory—that vain old biddy—cannot resist pencilling in a *few* slight cosmetic revisions in the margins of our past, making them revisionist recollections intended to reflect to the world the very best versions of our very false selves—masquerades meant to disguise our secret self-loathing and desperate desire to be loved by anyone, and approved by everyone, at any cost.

One Halloween when my daughter was small, she wanted me to wear a costume when I answered the door to greet the trick-or-treaters. The problem was, she got this idea on

Halloween morning. I told her it was too late for me to put anything together. "I know who you can be," she said brightly, disappearing from the breakfast table mysteriously. A few minutes later she dragged in the costume I wore when giving workshops on Victorian family celebrations.

"You can be Mrs. Sharp, Mommy."

Her father looked up from the newspaper, smiled, and said, "Whoa, Katie. The perfect mother. Now that's *really* scary."

Of course, he was right. Perfection is probably one of the most frightening of all the masquerades women wear, and not just at Halloween. Even our most cherished image of perfection—Home—has turned into something sinister and macabre, giving rise to a culture that worships domestic goddesses, whom we have unconsciously allowed to become graven images that diminish rather than enrich our creative life at home.

Ever since Eve bit the apple and lost Paradise for us, her daughters down through the ages have turned to goddesses for intercession and inspiration in order to finagle our way back. Greek women looked to Hestia, the goddess of the hearth. Roman women also had a hearth goddess they called Vesta. She was the one who urged women to be quiet, to sit, to gaze, to listen, to prepare delicious meals, to bring beauty into their daily round, to live through their senses, to create a sacred haven of security and serenity set apart from the greed and corruption of ancient Rome. Vesta was the goddess who called on women to focus their creative energies on what was Real.

In her book on ancient women's spirituality, *Classical*

Living: Reconnecting With the Rituals of Ancient Rome, Frances
Bernstein notes that the Latin word for hearth is *focus.* If you
think it was difficult for a woman to focus in ancient Roman
times, what about today when—in every moment of every
day—our time, creative energy, and emotions rush to fulfill
the inexhaustible demands of family and work?

The faster we run, the more conflicted we become. It's
been my experience that as soon as you realize you're getting
nowhere fast, you lose all clarity and focus because you're
hysterical; next you're experiencing an out-of-body phe-
nomenon that's confusing and disorienting. How many
times during the day do we speak about being "out of kilter,"
"spaced out," or "off the wall"? We use these phrases
because that's exactly how we feel; because we've wandered
too far away from our sacred center—the heart of our
House of Belonging—both physically and literally.

In order to regain our focus, we need to restore a sense of
soul to our home, which is what we're really trying to do
when we celebrate the accomplishments of domestic goddesses. We want our home to be the most beautiful spot on
earth. We long for our own everyday Eden. But glorifying
women whose public careers exploit our private yearnings
isn't the way to do it. Yes, I know, it's far easier to live vicar-
iously through their books, videos, magazines, newsletters,
television shows, websites, products, workshops, or even
infomercials than it is to nurture our own creative talents.
Vesta knows, I've tried.

And the reason we don't nurture our own Creatrix, our

own Divinity, is because when we do, whatever the domestic goddesses do looks better! Theirs is perfect—as well it should with expertly trained staff to do everything for them. It was touching when Martha Stewart returned from her private sojourn of several months getting in touch with her inner humility and publicly thanked her 600-member staff who so brilliantly and beautifully toiled in her name and absence. If it hadn't been for the news headlines, would we even have known she wasn't on the scene?

Wonder how your favorite cooking goddess always has another perfect casserole ready to show you as it emerges, bubbling, from the cauldron? Excuse me, oven. Well, it could be considered some form of witchcraft, because what you're watching on television is a form of magic. But it's not spells or incantations in the supernatural world the domestic goddesses rely on; it's personal and prop assistants, stylists, designers, and the best photographers on earth. That's why it looks picture-perfect. It's created by professionals.

Did you know that the food photographed in some lush magazine spreads is not even edible? It's so enhanced, lacquered, and tarted up, you'd do yourself bodily harm if you tried to eat it. But it looks perfect. Meanwhile, our soufflé, curtain treatment, kitchen potager, stencilled rug, knitted scarf, or crocheted blue poncho doesn't. So if we can't get it perfect, why bother?

The neurosis of perfectionism is feminine self-loathing disguised as self-improvement. It's an insidious, invisible addiction that's difficult to recognize because perfection is culturally sanctioned and socially approved; the pursuit of perfection allows us to run away from our pain and problems but be in plain view, fully present, and looking fabulous to the rest of the world. Some obsessions are more photogenic than others and perfectionism is a cover girl.

Perfection is also a brazen hussy, a clever slut known by many other names. At work her alias is *getting it right; fixing things; tinkering; revising; micromanaging; quality control; high performance; star quality.* On the couch we say she's being *anal-retentive, obsessive-compulsive,* suffering from *bulimia nervosa,* or *attention deficit syndrome.* At home it's having *great style, impeccable taste, that certain something. A good thing.*

Actually, perfectionism is *none* of these. So why don't we call the bitch what she really is: *perpetual care.* A size 2 shroud. Glamorous, designer-clad self-abuse. I'm sorry I have to be the little piggy squealing all the way home, but someone's got to say it: *domestic goddesses are bad for your health*, especially women care-aholics who perpetually tend to everything and everybody except themselves.

There, by the Grace of Mother Courage, do you and I both go today. When admiration leads to adoration of human beings and not of Spirit, we disown our birthright—our sacred passion. We siphon off our spiritual power by trading our own portion of creativity for that of a self-appointed expert whose judgment we trust more than our own. Is this what the expression "the rich get richer and the poor get poorer" means? Being poor in self-confidence and creative energy will keep you down-and-out quicker than a lean purse.

Images of airbrushed perfection saturate our culture through advertising, the media, and the entertainment industry. One of the most wonderful programs Oprah Winfrey has ever done (and there are 20 years' worth to choose from) was the one when she showed us all what she looks like when she wakes up; it's womanly, soft, comforting, appealing, and Real—not airbrushed. Yes, she looks gorgeous and polished on television; we would too. Besides, we want her to look splendiferous. It makes us happy to watch her being glorious. And do you know why? Because Oprah is our mentor, a role model, a sister. Oprah wants us to live *our* best lives, not hers.

The pursuit of perfection—perpetual care—is a powerful opiate of choice for millions of women who don't do heroin, crack, or pot; it's been mine, my entire life. It was also my mother's and, I've got to admit, a favorite obsession of almost every woman I know. Unfortunately, I don't know of any residential rehabs that specialize in kicking this habit, except the House of Belonging. As the beloved Julia Child so succinctly put it: "The tomato hides its griefs. Internal damage is hard to spot."

Just out of curiosity, how many glossy women's magazines do you have piled up to flip through for inspiration? Mine go back to the premiere issue of the late, much-loved, and long-lamented *Victoria* (Autumn 1987). I have the complete set; considering what individual issues are going for now on eBay, I probably should list my archive on my homeowner's insurance policy. But when I glance back through the pages of *Victoria,* I have to say that the fantasies depicted on its pages seem tame—more Sandra Dee in a ruffled, high-neck blouse than the sardonic cynicism being dished up today as empowerment. I don't think that any reader of *Victoria* ever really believed she could live like that. In fact, I was once on a photo shoot and heard a stylist comment, "Perfect! They'll *never* be able to do this at home!"

As long as we're on the topic of slick, sophisticated packaging and the growth industry that sells feminine insecurities so that from the bedroom to the kitchen there isn't one flaw we can't or won't turn against ourselves, how huge is that stack of unread self-help books next to your bed? No need to answer, sweetie, for I've come today to comfort, not to chide. But I'm going to need another brownie with that coffee refill to fuel my courage. Cream? Oh yes, please.

Bet you can't top this. A few years ago I was at an awards party for motivational books with my literary agent. We were sipping glasses of wine and surreptitiously glancing at all the titles nominated for the different awards. There were so many quick-fix books by the domestic goddesses about how to dress, decorate, "handle" relationships, manage money, halve your weight in a week, raise geniuses, and achieve organic orgasms that I started to swoon just looking at the stacks of them. We were also surrounded by complete strangers, most of them the authors, agents, and publishers of said enlightenment volumes. I had just muttered to Chris, "Who in the world *buys this stuff?*" when the editor of an inspirational book club rushed over and gleefully gushed in front of everybody that *I* was their **best** customer! Could I make this up? I was so mortified, I had to just brazen it through. So I said the first thing that came to mind about needing to "see" everything to stay on top of my publishing speciality, and then, small mercy, we were all told to take our seats.

In my favorite scene from the original *The Stepford Wives* movie, the circuitry of one of the robot-women (brilliantly and hilariously played by Nanette Newman) goes screwy at a garden party. All she can keep saying to everyone is "I'll die if I don't get that recipe." Remember that line the next time you're tempted, as I am again and again, by the lure of perfecting anything. Like salmonella lurking in the sour cream dip, perfection cleverly and convincingly cloaks her insidious intentions in party frocks—meant to be inspiration. But, babe, the stomach cramps that come when you just can't live up to your own impossible expectations are nastier than food poisoning.

MUCH DEPENDS ON HOMEMAKERS

Since Eve ate apples, much depends on dinner.
—George Gordon, Lord Byron

About the same time that Betty Friedan declared war on the American homemaker, another writer, the Pulitzer Prize-winning poet Phyllis McGinley, felt that she had to defend that honorable calling. "So highly do I regard our profession and its importance to the human scheme, it seems to me occupation sufficient to fill a life, a heart," she writes in her home memoir, *Sixpence in Her Shoe*. "One would think we should be constantly counting over our good fortune like beads."

I do, especially when I am in my kitchen. Writing from the trenches in 1964, Phyllis McGinley thought that the kitchen wouldn't come into its own again until it ceased to be a battlefield or a status symbol. "It may be pastel. It may be ginghamed as to curtains and shining with copper like a picture in a woman's magazine. But you and I will know it chiefly by its fragrances and its clutter. At the back of the stove will sit a soup kettle, gently bubbling, one into which every day are popped leftover bones and vegetables to make stock for sauces or soup for the family. Carrots and leeks will sprawl on counters, greens in a basket. There will be something sweet-smelling twirling in a bowl and something savory baking in the oven. Cabinet doors will gape ajar and colored surfaces are likely to be littered with salt and pepper and flour and herbs and cheesecloth and potholders and long-handled forks. It won't be neat. It won't even be efficient. But when you enter it you will feel the pulse of life throbbing from every corner. The heart of the home will have begun once again to beat."

But I wouldn't bother with Cream Mongole with Sherry, if I were you. My husband says my mom has much to answer for, and this is the proof of it. Blessed am I among women for the connection of past and present. I am, once again, my mother's daughter.

DO TRY THIS AT HOME:
LARDER LUST

*Tomatoes and oregano make it Italian; wine and
tarragon make it French. Sour cream makes it
Russian; lemon and cinnamon make it Greek. Soy
sauce makes Chinese; garlic makes it good.*

—Alice May Brock

And if you had a can of Italian tomatoes, oregano,
wine, tarragon, sour cream, lemon, cinnamon, soy
sauce, and garlic on hand, waiting for the moment inspiration stirred, you could make dinner any way you liked
tonight. I don't want to get too personal, but can you
remember the last time you tasted something so scrumptious
that the first bite triggered a squeal of delight, shivers of
pleasure, and spontaneous prayer? *Oh, my God, this is good!*
There's a reason the Bible tells us to "Taste and see how good
the Lord is."

That long, toots? And where was this epicurean
epiphany? At a fabulous place where you paid someone
to cook for you? Yes, that counts—but only if you tried to
recreate that savory or sweet sensation again in your
own kitchen.

And when was the last time you walked into the heart of
your home and concocted something yummy that tasted like

love to your tummy? Even longer? Well, it would seem that Divine intervention is the *plat du jour.* "Give us this day, our daily taste," as the poet Robert Farrar Capon asks on our behalf. Hey, we're big girls now; let's ask for ourselves.

It's unavoidably true that our senses become jaded as we get older—requiring new, fresh, and frequent jolts to awaken them and rouse us once more with feeling. Every adult has about ten thousand taste buds in the mouth (primarily on the tongue, but also on the palate, pharynx, and tonsils). Throughout our lives, every ten days or so, these taste buds wear out and regenerate. Unfortunately once we enter middle age, they don't regenerate as frequently as we might hope. This could be taken as a bitter pill, but I think of it as a cause for celebration. It gives me one more reason to stock another new-to-me taste sensation on my fancy pantry shelves.

You say you don't have a fancy pantry?

You do now. Or, at least, you will by the weekend.

"It's time to change the relationship between you and your kitchen. How would your kitchen feel if it was the person you lived with? When did you last make time for each other? Be honest with yourself because I mean real, quality time. Not just nipping in and out to put the kettle on. Not just over cereal in the morning when you are all sleepy and grumpy. And definitely not popping something ready-made into the oven and gawping at the telly," English cook and food writer Tom Norrington-Davies good-naturedly chides us in *Cupboard Love: How to Get the Most Out of Your*

Kitchen. "Let's face it. Your relationship with your kitchen has got to the point where you only really make an effort when there are others around. And do you remember the last time the two of you had people over? It was supposed to be a fun night but it got a bit stressful. You got positively scratchy with one another. You resented having to do all that last-minute shopping when you were the one out earning all day. You felt you made all the effort and never got to relax with your friends. An angry little part of you felt that your kitchen was cramping your style. It's not as if you haven't tried to spice things up a bit. You bought all the right books and (admit it) a fair few gadgets. You even bought your kitchen a fantastic makeover a couple of years back. There was gleaming stainless steel everywhere, but the sad truth is your relationship [with your kitchen] has gone 'off the boil'."

Well, we can take each other for better or worse, and in the best relationships we do both, just so long as we don't take each other for granted. Time to rekindle the culinary romance with a little cupboard love.

There is something so nourishing and nurturing about the notion of proper pantries and well-stocked larders—a continuing link of reconnection and restoration with preservation, the comfort of all that was good in the past, and the reassurance we need every day now. A century ago women didn't agonize over food the way contemporary middle-class American and British women do; sadly, we rarely take pleasure in eating and this emotional flatline is evident in the way we store our food. Think of Mrs. Bridges in

Masterpiece Theatre's *Upstairs, Downstairs*—a big, healthy, hearty, hardworking, handsome woman with a lusty appetite whose kitchen was certainly a sacred space. Yes, the very rich, upper class Bellamy family gave her carte blanche when stocking her well-ordered shelves, but if you remember, the folks downstairs ate as well as those fortunate enough to be invited to the dining room table. Mrs. Bridges had no ambivalence about enjoying one of life's Divinely appointed blessings—she loved food, she loved to cook, and so her pleasure blessed everyone else in her household. Her simply abundant larder proves that pride can't truly be a sin. A specially designed room off the kitchen with one outside wall and ventilation groaned with meat, fish, and fowl—not just baked or roasted but potted, brandied, and smoked; cheeses stored on cold slate shelves; freshly churned butter and eggs; and dry ingredients—flour, sugar, salt, rice, oats, and bran—stored in burlap sacks. Her pantry shelves held glistening jars of jams, jellies, conserves, fruited honeys, marmalades, mustards, chutneys, the pickles and nuts, including herbal marinades and remedies. There were tins for bread, cakes, pies, scones, and biscuits. Willow baskets would hold apples, pears, and seasonal fruit, such as apricots, peaches, and plums, as well as root vegetables with the goodness of the earth still clinging to them.

Since antiquity there have been forbidden foods. From the apple to aphrodisiacs, certain foods have always been associated with danger and risk. However, in recent years, all foods seem to have become suspect for one reason or another, because now we prize perfection and health over taste. Once a source of enchantment, food has now become a source of some entrapment. And while our cholesterol levels have never been lower, so are our spirits. "The soul needs to be fattened," Thomas Moore advises us in his exquisite contemplation of the sacred in the ordinary, *The Re-Enchantment of Everyday Life.* "The idea of feeding the soul is an old one, which can be found in mystical literature from around the world." And he's not referring to cookbooks, but holy canons.

Would that I could bless you, myself, and every woman reading this book with a walk-in larder and pantry. I can't add another room onto your homes, but I can encourage you to designate one cupboard as your fancy pantry.

First, let's bring order to the cupboards, your refrigerator, and freezer with a proper clearout. In the cupboard, anything past its *shelf life* (which means it's probably a couple of years old already) is ditched. I know there will be some people who argue that one should donate canned foods of any kind to homeless shelters or food banks, but I think this is odious. Spiritual tradition of every faith tells us to feed the hungry *better* than ourselves. So out those old tins go, and when you purchase a bottle of extra virgin olive oil and sea salt for your fancy pantry, if you're able, buy another to donate. The gratitude of the people working in shelter kitchens for the gift of quality condiments and staples is heart humbling and Soul nourishing.

Now to the refrigerator: Here we part with the half-eaten remnants of ancient cultures—yes, including the marmalade your sister-in-law brought back from London a decade ago. If you didn't finish it in a year, trust me, you're not going to get a craving to spread it on your toast now. Personally, I think keeping and consuming anything past its *sell by* date is dodgy, whether it has fuzz on it or not. As Mrs. Bridges used to say, if it smells like fish, throw it back. In the freezer: Speaking of the fishy, if you can't remember when you froze that tuna casserole, you know what to do. Ditto anything that's been frozen three months or more. It's tasteless by now and, yes, that matters.

The look we're actually going for in the kitchen right now is lean so we can begin again—and this time make a peace offering to our bodies and souls. We're going to start over from scratch and rediscover one of your sacred senses: taste. Many women, including me, swallow life in an attempt to keep it manageable. I mean this literally and figuratively. Whenever we're anxious, worried, nervous, or depressed, without thinking we instinctively swallow anything in reach in order to push away the uncomfortable, negative feelings our overwrought emotions are arousing within us. We don't taste, we don't savor, we don't revel, we don't appreciate, we don't give thanks; we just swallow.

It's no small blessing, sweetie, we don't need to keep rat poison handy in the kitchen anymore.

NESTING INSTINCTS:
SPICE GIRLS

Cooking is like love. It should be entered into with abandon or not at all.

—Harriet Van Horne

id you know that with few exceptions many of the spices we use today can be traced back to use in early human history? That for thousands of years spices have been as highly valued as international currency—beyond gold? Spices have created and destroyed empires, nourished people, cured illnesses, defined cuisines, preserved cultures, provoked wars, warded off evil spirits, and been used to worship benevolent ones. It was the pursuit of cinnamon, pepper, and nutmeg that sent Christopher Columbus westward to the Indies, Vasco da Gama eastward to Africa, and Ferdinand Magellan around the globe. None of them set out to find new worlds. It was new flavors and scents they were seeking.

Ah, chérie. Seems like old times again. You. Me. The Spice Girls. Those babes have come and gone, but what do you want to bet there's a box of Bell's Seasoning at the back of your cupboard older than their time together? I know, we cleared the spice rack a decade ago in *Simple Abundance*. Call me frivolous, I'll deny it.

First, open each container and give the spice a deep sniff; if the aroma is pungent, it can stay. But if a ground spice has fossilized or it smells like nothing, you know what to do. Crush an herb (rosemary, thyme...) between your fingers; if it smells grassy or dull, it's no longer potent and whatever you are cooking will only be as good as the foodstuffs you use.

Next, pull all the jars, bottles, and cans out and put them on the kitchen table. Pad and pen at the ready, weed out the ones you've never or rarely used; you'll recognize them by the dust. Put them to one side. No matter what the recipe calls for, you're not crazy about these taste sensations. Knowledge is power. Finally, sort out the sometimes-used cans or jars, then the frequently used ones. This seemingly pointless exercise provides immediate gratification.

Spices are still costly, so don't feel you have to replace everything. Instead, replace the spices you use regularly. The better the quality of your spices, the less you'll need, so think of them as affordable luxuries. And all spices lose their flavor after a year, so always buy the smallest quantities available if the seasoning is new to you. I have had wonderful creative excursions shopping for unusual ones at ethnic food markets. Behold! See the camel caravans slowly making their way across the heat and dust. If you listen imaginatively, you can hear the traders haggling over the prices in the exotic port of Dar es Salaam. A sailor returns from a long voyage and brings his sweetheart a small fragrant package. She slowly opens it and inhales the deep aroma of his love. Why did he take such a risk? Her love is worth it, he reassures her, knowing her love will soon be the cardamom cake he'll be taking with him on his next journey. But even Chinese empresses, Arabian princes, and Indian maharajas reserved these green seed pods for special occasions— love offerings. Biting on cardamom pods was Cleopatra's way of making her mouth irresistible. Try it. Come on, I see you smiling. That's the way you're supposed to feel in your kitchen. My work seems to be done in this room, but may your pleasure only be unfolding.

Did you know that making love is the only endeavor to simultaneously engage and excite all seven of a woman's sacred senses: sight, sound, scent, touch, taste, knowing, and wonder? That's because love makes all things new.

So for the love of all that's holy, Woman, get thy spice rack in order and praise to Heaven be, for Paradise found.

HEART REFLECTIONS:
THE BELOVED INVOKES HEAVEN FOR SUSTENANCE AND GRACE

Blessed Mother Courage, Holy Provider of the Feast, the warmth of your hearth and the simple Abundance of your celebrating table bid me Welcome. I enter into Thy Shelter of Nurturance with True Thanksgiving. Hear the prayer of Your Beloved, who asks with a humble heart that her long days of self-deprivation may end. May she find solace and sustenance in her House of Belonging. Bless her famished heart and wilted Spirit, and release her ravaged body from the cruel addiction of self-abuse: the pursuit of perfection, the denial of pleasure, the suppression of her sacred sense of taste.

Grandmother of Ancient Memory, cradle your child at your breast, hear, and hush her earliest cries of hunger and thirst. Sustainer of Life, travel back with her perishing soul to the first moment of this life when her holy needs as a child were unmet and her sacred wants denied. May the words of our prayer reverse this unnatural thwarting of your Divine Plan for her happiness. Begin this day a new, blessed reconciliation between her hungry heart and your Divine gift of food. Give her this day one day's portion of Grace that she might be awakened to the ecstasy of her passionate palate and the Everyday Eden awaiting in her blessed Yummy Kitchen.

Reveal to your Beloved the Divine Mystery whispered in Eve's ear in reassurance and not abandonment, which enabled the first woman to cultivate the fruits of the Good Earth and bring forth abundance. Restore to your Divine Daughter one blessed ingredient, one sensuous spice, one seductive aroma, one tantalizing recipe, one mouthwatering bite, one delicious day at a time, all the joys of Paradise waiting to be reclaimed.

Bless this wonderful woman, in her sacred space we pray. May she always sip from the Cup of Good Cheer and partake with thanksgiving from Divine Provisions of Your Luscious Larder those love offerings that have been set aside for her and her alone, since the very thought of her earthly pleasure brought a smile to Heaven's countenance. May Thy glorious gifts now and always gladden her own heart.

Be it done, with all praise and honor according to Thee, and accepted most gratefully by She.

CHAPTER SEVEN

DWELLING IN THE HOUSE OF SPIRIT

ON EVERYDAY EPIPHANIES AND PRIVATE PILGRIMAGES

> *I shall not tell you in this story about all the days when nothing happened. You will not catch me saying, "thus the sad days passed slowly by"—or "the years rolled on their weary course," or "time went on"—because it is silly; of course time goes on, whether you say so or not.*

—Edith Nesbit

*W*hen I was in my twenties I lived in London and became incredibly curious about the world of spirits. Not God, mind you, but the lower spiritual realm—

divination—which is seeking to know the future or hidden things through supernatural powers. As I really didn't know too many people in England, I started hanging out with the wrong crowd because they asked me to pay them a visit, literally: spiritualists, psychics, mediums, tarot card readers, astrologers. Not that all these people were bad; they were just bad for me. I did meet a few charlatans who weren't interested in my destiny or soul—just the money they could extract by manipulating my misery. But if a gypsy in a turban and gold hoop earrings who sees "clients" in a fringed silk tent in the middle of an antique market consults her crystal ball and tells you to put a raw egg underneath your bed, to pay her the equivalent of a month's rent, and to give her the gold bangle bracelet you got for your 21st birthday as a "seed offering" and you do it, as I did, you can bet that your future's going to include a stinky apartment, a pissed-off landlady, an empty wallet, a barren wrist, and disillusionment.

What did I expect? Well, at 25 I expected *everything*, especially the instant answer to my very reasonable prayers, which were for love, money, and fame. *Now.* As Edna Ferber wrote about a young woman in her 1926 novel, *Show Boat,* I wanted to know only one thing: " 'What about her Future?' Future, as she pronounced it, was spelled with a capital *F* and was a thin disguise for the word husband."

So I continued my restless, relentless search for someone to tell me what I desperately wanted to hear. I wasn't just addicted to Love; I was addicted to Destiny—especially my version of it. After months of waiting, I finally got a reading with a famous English psychic who told me I would spend the next 30 years waiting for my soul mate. "This life is about seeking as much as it is finding. But what you find won't only be priceless for you but for many others."

Thirty years? I was aghast.

"Maybe 25…" he hedged, seeing the desperation on my face. "But he must be a *very* important man," the psychic tried to reassure me. "Because I sense the word *Abundance* surrounding you in many languages. I feel such an outpouring of gratitude for your path. So many blessings flowing through you and around you. What a wonderful life you're going to have in … hmmm … about 25 years."

Good Lord. Stop right now. If this guy was right I'd be over 50 before true love found me. Well, what do psychics know anyway? Naturally, to resist crawling out on the nearest ledge, I had to put my own positive spin on this devastating news. A couple bottles of wine later I'd interpreted the prediction to mean that, like Rita Hayworth, I'd marry the Aga Khan or an international financier. At the very least, I'd spend my dotage in luxurious comfort.

Wrong again. No Far Eastern potentate on bended knee. But how freaky-deeky that two decades after that prediction, I wrote *Simple Abundance*, which has been published in languages that span the globe.

Finally, I had to stop seeking the advice of seers and start seeking Spirit. I'm very thankful that many of the predictions made in my twenties came true in rather astonishing ways—*but decades later.* Divine Timing is completely different from ours, but it's never late—and always perfect. Probably just not tomorrow. It took a long, long time for me to accept the Soul knowledge that when we wait for a future others have foretold, we return to Spirit the gift waiting for us today—the present. For this I tell you, and it's very true: When you seek and follow the personal prompts of your authentic self—your Soul made visible—your good fortune in life, love, and real estate is assured, here and now.

LAST CALL

> We have lost so many leaves
> In loss, loss, loss
> Out of the sky,
> What shall we do for shelter to live by?
>
> —Josephine Miles

There were many things that impacted upon me after September 11, 2001, that made me look at my life and the choices I'd made in the years following my divorce. Certainly they were exciting years; I traveled a great deal and loved most of it. Writing other books and setting up the Simple Abundance Charitable Fund was very rewarding. And I created two very different and appealing homes on either side of the Atlantic. But the photographs in my upstairs hallway tell the real story: pictures of Katie and me in a gondola in Venice; Katie and me at an Oscar party in Los Angeles; Katie and me in Colorado white-water rafting; Katie and me at the Eiffel Tower. Oh, there was the occasional event at which my teenager wasn't my date. But in the end, no matter which home I'd return to, I would go to sleep alone.

Perhaps that's why the last call so many people in the Twin Towers and on the planes made to loved ones to say good-bye had such an impact on me. Last calls to say "I love you," last calls to say "Don't forget me," last calls to say "I'll be with you always," and a last call to say, as one man told his wife, his soul mate, "I will find you again."

While surely my last calls would include my cherished daughter, it still made me so sad that, after a lifetime of believing and searching for my "last call" partner, I hadn't found him. Because I know with all my heart and soul that once upon my last lifetime, I made someone that promise: "I will find you again."

That autumn of 2001 I remained in New York until Christmas. Just the thought of being an ocean away from Katie was unbearable. The apartment on Central Park West became our refuge, our soul shelter, and with every turn of the key, our home. Our House of Belonging.

But it was very difficult to concentrate, let alone write—and writing is what paid my bills. I was supposed to be working on *Romancing the Ordinary* at the time, a celebration of a woman's seven senses (the five physical ones and the two spiritual—*knowing* and *wonder*). In other words, a happy romp through the pleasures of every day. However, you could not walk down a street in Manhattan without passing at least one makeshift shrine, and for months there were funerals all over the city, all day long.

A profound pall shrouded the city. To smile or laugh at anything but dark, gallows humor felt inappropriate.

All I wanted to do was lose myself in the anonymity—disguise my private fears behind the enormity of the public loss, even though no one I knew personally was missing or killed. What made this plan impossible was that I was being asked to appear on television shows to give comfort, advice, and solace; I was also being asked to write reassuring magazine features on what good could come out of all this disaster.

On the days I didn't have to be a public person, I kept to a simple schedule. In the morning, I would straighten my drawers and closets and make lists of their contents; in the afternoon I finally used a birthday gift certificate for riding lessons at the Central Park stables or delivered cases of soft drinks we donated to the volunteers at Ground Zero. Other days I'd find myself sitting on a bench with a cup of coffee just staring at the stunning blue sky and white clouds, mesmerized by the trees, which hadn't turned autumnal but remained leafy and green until December. Not only had the world been caught up short by terrorism, it seemed, but Mother Nature had been as well.

Unless I was going out with Katie, my evenings were solitary and sacrosanct—and homebound. Every evening at 6 p.m. I would prepare a different pasta recipe (from the one cookbook I had in New York) and decant a decent bottle of red wine. (I reasoned, if you weren't going to start drinking good wine on your own when the world was blowing up, then it was never going to happen.) Then I'd arrange a pleasing dinner tray and take it to my bedroom, which was at the farthest end of the apartment. Once ensconced under my comfy duvet, wearing my favorite Victoria's Secret jersey pajamas and Lands' End gray cashmere sweater robe (which I still wear) and socks, I'd eat dinner in bed while watching old black and white films, particularly ones with World War II themes. My favorite was the 1942 Oscar-winning wartime saga, *Mrs. Miniver,* starring Greer Garson. Directed by William Wyler, it depicts an English middle-class family's heroic struggle to preserve what was precious in their daily life during the London Blitz before America entered the war.

MYTHICAL WOMEN

> *Linking our personal story to the great web and patterns of those who have traveled that path before can significantly alleviate the aloneness and confusion that often plague the modern woman. Myths show us what our stories have in common.*

> —Sheryl Paul Nissinen

Have you ever lost yourself so completely in a book or a movie that you became part of it? Something about the story, the writer's voice, the heroine, or the conversations in the dialogue strikes a profound mystical chord in you. A timeless echo of enchantment reverberates. That's because the story is a retelling of your personal myth.

Each of us has a personal myth. It's a story as old as time, but it's *your* story. From ancient times, myths and fairy tales have contained more spiritual truth in one telling than we can even begin to process, which is why the soul keeps seeking it through different media—books, film, theater, art, and history. Remember how Jesus told stories or parables to the crowds that followed him? He was using their daily round to help them understand the sacred in their own ordinary lives—the seed that falls on rocky ground; the shepherd who protects his flock; the lilies of the field, who neither toil nor spin but are exquisitely dressed; the lost coin in the household; the hidden treasure in the empty lamp; the ingredients in preparing a meal.

Like the spiritual gift of intuition and the intimate resonance of the Deeper Vibration, our personal myth is a sacred compass to guide us from danger to safety through life's labyrinth when we are lost. "Remember that the imagination is the faculty of the soul," the Irish writer Caitlin Matthews reminds us, "and that when it suggests new pathways to us we are being invited to explore the territory of the soul in ways that will certainly change and re-enchant us." Unearthing our personal myth is one of these imaginative ways our Soul communicates with us. The way you've weathered crises, taken risks, made choices, or overcome challenges has been determined, in large part, by your belief system, which includes the people you admire most, whether they're living or dead, fictional or historical.

"Women, I believe, search for fellow beings who have faced similar struggles," the distinguished author and critic Carolyn G. Heilbrun observes in *Writing A Woman's Life*.

She is referring to the kinship that develops between readers and writers and one she shared with the poet Maxine Kumin, a close friend "only in my mind" and between the lines of Kumin's poetry. "Why do I feel, not having met her but having read all her work, that she and I are closer in the destinies we have chosen than I am to many friends personally known?"

I know exactly what she means. Do you? While every woman needs flesh-and-blood confidants, there are some times when your chosen circle have no frame of reference in their own experiences to help you navigate your way through the unexpected shock and rocky shoals of change.

During those terror-heightened months when I felt so inept at giving advice to others, I needed a woman in my life who I could emulate; one who possessed "repose of the soul." A woman who delighted in my passion for domesticity and reveled in her feminine wiles. A grown-up woman to help me remember what mattered most—making a safe haven in a scary and tumultuous world for my daughter and myself. A woman who had built her own House of Belonging: Mrs. Miniver.

Think of movies as celluloid myths told to a culture no longer sitting around a campfire but in front of a screen. "Movies elevate our sights, enlarge our imagination. Film, like poetry, is one of our heart's most subtle agents. It reminds us of what we know, helps us stretch and change," Marsha Sinetar suggests in her fascinating book *Reel Power*: *Spiritual Growth Through Film*. "Their themes and images can powerfully equip us to see ourselves as we are, at our worst, and at our best, or to help us invent new scripts about who we hope to be.... Certain films—like certain lovely people, glorious works of art or music, and special instances of prayer—seem a grace expressly given for our edification."

BECOMING MRS. MINIVER

We find what we search for—or, if we don't find it we become it.

—Jessamyn West

Dearest Reader, meet Kay Miniver. Many people think they already know Mrs. Miniver because they've seen the film. However, before Greer Garson so beautifully embodied Mrs. Miniver on the screen, she was a newspaper figment of British journalist Jan Struther's domestic reveries featured in the *London Times* between 1937 and 1939. Known for her stylish prose, witty poems, and modern hymns, Jan had been asked by her editor to write "about an ordinary sort of woman who leads an ordinary sort of life—rather like yourself."

Charm makes everyone feel better, and during this time, threats of war were daily headlines in Britain. Mrs. Miniver's contagious zest for dashing "through life at full tilt, with gaiety, energy, and grace" captivated readers' imaginations. "It was lovely, thought Mrs. Miniver, nodding good-bye to the flower-woman and carrying her big sheaf of chrysanthemums down the street with a kind of ceremonious joy, as though it were a cornucopia; it was lovely, this settling down again, the tidying away of the summer into its box, this taking up of the thread of one's life where the holidays (irrelevant interlude) had made one drop it. Not that she didn't enjoy the holidays; but she always felt—and it was, perhaps, a measure of her peculiar happiness—a little relieved when they were over. Her normal life pleased her so well that she was half afraid to step out of the frame in case one day she should find herself unable to get back. The spell might break, the atmosphere be impossible to recapture."

Nothing in Mrs. Miniver's daily round was too insignificant that it couldn't become an uplifting source of reflection, revelation, reconnection, and renewal, and she reminded readers how much they had to be grateful for in the small particulars of everyday epiphanies: the familiar route to a holiday home; unread library books to look forward to; the comforting feel of the banister beneath your hand as you climbed the stairs; having another's hand to hold and eye to catch at a dinner party; the small indentation at the nape of your child's neck, so perfect for a quick kiss; the pang of parting from the old family car; finding the perfect calendar to give pleasure throughout the year; the notches on the nursery door as the children grew; a hat with a floppy bow; the mingling scent of roses and a fire in the hearth; crumpets for tea on a rainy afternoon.

"Perhaps you might call this the testament of a happy woman," the American writer Christopher Morely wrote in the American Book of the Month Club edition of Jan

Struther's essays published in October 1939 (as *Mrs. Miniver*) just after World War II broke out in Europe. Mrs. Miniver's musings on "eternity wrapped in domesticity" became a best seller on both sides of the Atlantic and a powerful force for popularizing America's entry into the war.

English Prime Minister Winston Churchill predicted that *Mrs. Miniver*'s contribution to the war effort would be more important than the flotilla of warships he'd been begging (in vain) for American President Franklin D. Roosevelt to send to Britain, and he was right. Six months after Pearl Harbor, in June 1942, after *Mrs. Miniver* premiered at Radio City Music hall to a sobbing audience, Winston Churchill got his ships. President Roosevelt was so moved and stirred by the closing scene, a sermon delivered by the vicar in a bombed-out church, that he had the text broadcast over Voice of America in Europe and printed on millions of leaflets which were dropped over German-occupied territory.

The homes of many of us have been destroyed, and the lives of young and old have been taken. There is scarcely a household that hasn't been struck to the heart.

And why? Surely you must have asked yourself this question. Why in all conscience should these be the ones to suffer? Children, old people, a young girl at the height of her loveliness. Why these? Are these our soldiers? Are these our fighters? Why should they be sacrificed?

I shall tell you why.

Because this is not only a war of soldiers in uniform. It is a war of the people, of all the people, and it must be fought not only on the battlefield, but in the cities and in the villages, in the facto-ries and on the farms, in the home, and the heart of every man, woman, and child who loves freedom!.... This is the people's war! It is our war! We are the fighters! Fight it then! Fight it with all that is in us, and may God defend the right.

THE HOME FRONT

> The main figure in the Home Front is the woman. It is she who must make the stand, rally her family around her like a general, and plant her own feet firmly on the home ground. Everything depends on her wisdom, her enthusiasm, her vision of what home can produce, what home can be.
>
> —Harper's Bazaar, May 1942

When a book or movie strikes the same chord in millions of people, it is the work of Spirit, even if it springs from a human heart, mind, and hands. "Myth is the revelation of divine life in man [or woman]," the great Swiss psychologist Carl Jung believed. "It is not we who invent myth, rather it speaks to us as a Word of God." *Mrs. Miniver* was such a Divine inspiration—the embodiment of a sacred archetype of a woman defending her family and home from all danger through her faith, intelligence, strength, courage, determination, unshakable optimism, and love. And it is such a powerful myth precisely because each of us can see ourselves in that role. Mrs. Miniver was a wife who reveled in being married, a mother who cherished her children and adored her home. Unfortunately both Greer Garson and Jan Struther, the creator of *Mrs. Miniver,* found their personal lives eclipsed by trying to live up to this myth. Although both women tried in vain to explain that they were not Mrs. Miniver, the world would not see them otherwise.

One wonders how Mrs. Miniver's fans would have reacted if they had known that at the time of making the movie, Greer Garson, then 33, was having an affair with the actor, Richard Ney, who played her college-aged son in the movie. Hollywood mogul Louis B. Mayer persuaded both of them to wait until after the movie's first run before getting married, which they did, but it only lasted four years. Fifty years later, Greer Garson would say, "Graciousness has haunted me my whole life."

Jan Struther's private life was the darkest caricature of her creation, as different as day and night. Imagine living up to this compliment from the *St. Petersburg (Fla.) Times* found among Jan Struther's personal papers after she died: "Of Mrs. Miniver's philosophy, one can truly say that she has found the true art of living, the art of loving, the art of marriage, the art of family life, the art of happiness. There are no triangular love affairs, not an indecent suggestion. It is a book any granddaughter can safely put in the hands of her grandmother."

But the truth was that by 1939 Jan Struther's marriage was deeply in trouble, for she had fallen in love with a much younger man, a Jewish intellectual who had fled from Nazi-occupied Vienna to live in the United States. Under the cover of bringing her two younger children to safety in

America, she followed him to New York, where she would remain during the war, carrying on a clandestine affair with him while her husband was a British POW. After the war ended and her husband returned home, Jan Struther divorced and finally, in 1948, she married Dolf Placzek. However, the incalculable strain of the secrecy, stress, and guilt Jan carried, along with the burden of pretending she was the perfect embodiment of saintly womanhood for years, contributed to a nervous breakdown, a five-month stay at a psychiatric sanatorium, and a paralyzing depression before she died of breast cancer in 1953.

"I sometimes imagine the kind of grandmother she might have turned into, if she really had been the 'Mrs. Miniver' of her own creation," her granddaughter Ysenda Maxtone Graham writes in her immensely touching biography, *The Real Mrs. Miniver: Jan Struther's Story*. "She would have been one of those paper-thin, white-haired Chelsea ladies who live in mansion flats off the King's Road…. Her drawing room would have been a chintzy, scented haven of potpourri and lilies, with pink-and-white striped sofas and silver-framed photographs of her deceased husband in a kilt…. We would have sat together by the fire … and she would have talked about what the King's Road used to be like in the 1930s…. But Jan Struther never reached old age. She died at 52. Even if she had survived till her eighties, she wouldn't have been that kind of grandmother at all. She would have lived on the Upper West Side of Manhattan in an untidy apartment strewn with open reference books and long-playing records not put back into their sleeves. We would have sat by the air-conditioning unit, drinking gin and tonic out of chipped glasses and talking about love and politics."

Ysenda Maxtone Graham recounts that "during the height of *Mrs. Miniver*'s fame and success during the war, Jan toured America as an unofficial ambassadress for Britain, giving hundreds of lectures about Anglo-American relations to enchanted audiences. The public wanted to believe that she was the embodiment of her fictional creation—a sensible, calm, devoted wife and mother. She felt it was her wartime duty not to disappoint them. No one guessed ... that she was in fact living two parallel lives."

As her granddaughter reveals, the tragedy was that Jan Struther "had a remarkable capacity for writing important things down." But after the words were written, after the inspiration pierced the heart of the reader, after the inspiration became an icon, Jan Struther paid a price for accepting the mantle of martyrdom and the duty of self-sacrifice. By ignoring and denying what her granddaughter calls her "thorn-sharp" needs—the loves, lusts, and longings that are every woman's sacred hungers—hers was a short life that ended sorrowfully in "shudders and sighs."

THE SECOND TIME AROUND

*It is not a bad thing in a tale that you understand
only half of it.*

—Isak Dinesen

*I*n November 2002, I was returning to my home in Maryland after the first weekend of a lengthy publicity tour for *Romancing the Ordinary.* The plane had just landed and was taxiing to the gate when a man sitting behind me reached up with one arm to open the overhead compartment directly over me. Because he was in a rush, because he was inconsiderate, because he wasn't in the aisle where he should have been in order to safely retrieve his belongings, his heavy suitcase fell directly on my head. We think that lightning doesn't strike in the same place twice, but actually it frequently does.

In a coincidence that beggared belief, a large ceiling panel in a restaurant had fallen onto my head 18 years before. No one else in the restaurant was hit. Although I never lost consciousness, I sustained a concussion that left me bedridden, confused, and disoriented for months and partially disabled for a year and a half. During the first few months of my recuperation, my senses were all skewed. Ironically, the new book I was promoting, *Romancing the Ordinary,* was about my recovery and rediscovery of life all over again through each of my senses.

All rites of passage—getting married or divorced, finding a new job, becoming a parent or a grandparent, moving, changing careers, navigating midlife, financial setbacks, retirement, the death of a parent or a spouse, or adjusting to chronic illness—involve identity changes. A shedding of the old life, an altering of life patterns, and a readjustment of rhythm must occur before the new persona emerges. Remember? It's called transition.

The ordinary instant had struck again.

The difference between the two accidents was that with the first head injury I had only my own loss of livelihood to worry about in the months it took to get well; with the second one, I was also responsible for the livelihoods of my staff and maintaining two businesses. The burden was enormous and more than I, or any one person, was capable of carrying. Still, I pretended otherwise by using my personal savings and liquidating investments to keep up appearances and morale and to keep everyone else going until finally I couldn't afford the charade anymore. Despairing, I sold my house in Maryland, gave up my beautiful apartment on Central Park West, and closed down The Simple Abundance Press. My doctors recommended I return to Newton's Chapel to recover in private; I saw it as licking my wounds—physical, psychological, emotional, and financial. But I didn't want anyone to know how fragile I was. I felt I'd failed. I was ashamed and thought, just as I had when my marriage ended, that if people knew of my reversal of fortune, somehow it would be twisted and the truth of *Simple Abundance* would be undermined—that it would be thrown back in my face. I feared that all I had was *not* all I needed at the moment it counted the most. Yes, I'd taken too much on, but even when I'd seen the crack in the ice beneath my feet, I'd kept on skating. I was becoming Mrs. Miniver. I also secretly believed that the work I was doing in the world was making enough difference in women's lives to protect me from misfortune. What kind of hubris was this? Because it certainly couldn't protect me from myself.

"Magical thinking" is how Joan Didion poignantly nails the mind's Byzantine labyrinth as it tries to process shock, grief, and loss. "I was thinking as small children think, as if my thoughts or wishes had the power to reverse the narrative, change the outcome. In my case this disordered thinking had been covert, noticed I think by no one else, hidden even from me, but it had also been in retrospect, both urgent and constant. In retrospect there had been signs, warning flags I should have noticed."

I prayed to God to save me when the foundations of my house began to shake and when I looked up, hoping to find rescue, to my horror I realized it was God who was shaking down my house. If I couldn't save myself from the pursuit of perfection and the myth that was growing around *Simple Abundance*, then it was time for a spiritual time-out. Heaven wanted my complete attention, and this way Spirit got it.

THE HOUSE OF SPIRIT

August 1945: There was a time before the war—it seems in another world. Where has it gone? Am I the writer who wrote Black Narcissus? Has she gone, just as the money is gone? Is it possible I shall write again? First I must cope with England ... which has never seemed so alien.

—Rumer Godden

"To despair is traitorous to your gift," Rumer Godden admonishes. After weeks in bed in Newton's Chapel I finally started to read again. I began taking stock of my losses and felt very sorry for myself. I reached for favorite memoirs of women to comfort and console me.

"What were they thinking?" is a magazine and newspaper headline often used as a commentary over funny or bizarre photographs. But now I wanted to know what my heroines were thinking as they faced the challenges, crossroads, change, and choices that shaped the trajectory of their lives. How did they recover when sorrow slapped them down? How did they feel after achieving a long-desired dream, only to find that friends were too jealous to share their joy? How did they cope when suddenly their success turned to ashes?

My favorite, among many, was Rumer Godden's memoir, *A House With Four Rooms,* concerning the years between 1945–1977 after the huge success of her third novel, *Black Narcissus.* By the time it was made into a breathtaking color film (1946) starring Deborah Kerr as the Mother Superior of a small group of nuns trying to establish a mission in a remote Himalayan outpost, Rumer Godden was paying off debts left when her husband, a stockbroker whom she'd mistakenly trusted to invest her money safely, deserted her and their two children. I am mesmerized by how she lived, nurtured a family, and created many soul shelters—successive Houses of Belonging all over the world—while writing 57 books, including novels for both children and adults, nonfiction, short story collections, and poetry.

The secret she shares is that no matter where we actually keep house, we must daily dwell in the House of Spirit: "There is an Indian proverb or axiom that says that everyone is a house with four rooms, a physical, an emotional, a mental, and a spiritual. Most of us tend to live in one room most of the time, but unless we go into every room every day, even if only to keep it aired, we are not a complete person.... I have tried to go most days into them all—each has its riches."

BECAUSE YOU'RE WORTH IT

Every spirit builds itself a house, and beyond its house, a world, and beyond its world, a heaven. Know then that the world exists for you.

—Ralph Waldo Emerson

I know that you can have a wonderful husband, a happy marriage, and a loving family but still feel estranged from your surroundings, as if you're not living in your House of Belonging. Why is that, do you think?

Because the House of Belonging is not a place. It is a pres-ence—*your* authentic presence in *your* own life and *your* own home.

I love how Florida Pier Scott-Maxwell describes the refuge which comforted her after her first marriage ended. "After a time of trouble I found a likeable flat which was to be my home. I had had a long need of one, so it was also my dear shelter. My daughter and I moved in one evening with two suitcases, two beds, three pots of bulbs, a kettle and tea things. We lit a brilliant fire in the seemly little grate with the dry slats the builder had left after making a big opening between the two public rooms. I lay in the firelight peace-fully listening to pigeons on the roof.... I listened, looked out on the trees beyond both windows and I was free and happy.... It was already so precious to me that its surface was almost my skin."

Almost her skin. A home so alive and protective, it's as close as your own skin. She was, of course, describing her House of Belonging, though to the eyes of an outsider it was just a tiny apartment. She would go on to have other homes, including a large Scottish country house, but she knew then, as I know now (and soon it is my prayer that you will know too), that any shelter where you find comfort, contentment, safety, and refuge—however temporary it might be—is your House of Belonging.

However, if you've never been married before or don't have a live-in partner by the time your reach your 30s or 40s, there's a huge psychological and emotional barrier to your happiness—that is, whether or not you believe you're worthy enough to establish a "proper" home alone.

Please, dearest friend. *The House of Belonging is not an Ark, to be entered into only two by two.* In fact, as a spiritual directive, if you don't create, live in, love, and believe you're worthy of the soul shelter of your own House of Belonging *without* a partner, you'll never be happy *with* one.

Like many women, I've always admired Gloria Steinem. My admiration goes back to the days when she was writing beauty pieces for *Glamour* magazine in the '60s when I was in high school. To this day, I keep Q-tips in my silver baby cup because I read once that she did. Gloria has written affectingly of the search for personal redemption in her memoir, *Revolution from Within: A Book of Self-Esteem.* The renowned editor of *MS* magazine took on the role of family caregiver because her parents divorced when she was ten and her mother struggled with a debilitating depression. As an adult, this feminist inspiration and icon worked tirelessly for causes, but she didn't have a clue about taking care of herself—emotionally, psychologically, and physically. It just goes to prove in a powerful way that a woman does not have to be married and/or a mother to morph into a martyr. All her adult life she'd lived in an apartment she described as "a closet where I changed clothes and dumped papers into cardboard boxes."

Eventually, through a long, painful process of playing lost and found with Life, she gradually came to the belated awareness that one's home was a "symbol of the self" and in her 50s created and relished living in her first real home.

The 19th-century novelist Edith Wharton was in her 50s when she fell passionately in love with a house in the south of France. "I feel as if I were going to get married—to the right man at last!" she wrote about her beloved "Hyeres." More than 20 years before, in 1897, she'd coauthored (with Ogden Codman, Jr.) America's first best-selling interior decoration book, *The Decoration of Houses.* Although Edith Wharton would become renowned for the interior of her 35-room mansion in Lenox, Massachusetts, "The Mount"— America's first designer showcase—she never expressed the same depth of emotion or bond with any of her grand homes as she did with her modest House of Belonging.

Edith Wharton described a woman's nature like a huge house with rooms set aside for visitors and other rooms—the more comfortable ones—meant only for family and friends. "But beyond that, far beyond, are other rooms, the handles of whose doors are never turned ... and in the innermost room, the holy of holies, the soul sits alone and waits for a footstep that never comes."

All her life Edith Wharton would use the metaphor of houses and architectural places to explore belonging and entitlement, never quite making the connection that the footstep the Soul was waiting for was her own.

In *Around the House and In the Garden: A Memoir of Heartbreak, Healing, and Home Improvement,* Dominique Browning tells a story about a friend that is a cautionary tale

for all women of a certain age who haven't invested emotionally, psychologically, spiritually, or financially in feathering
their own nests. "What she wanted—what she had planned
on—was to fall in love, get married, and make a home with
someone. It wasn't happening, though." And although this
woman "was a person of accomplishment, fortitude, and
sophistication," as she entered her forties she began to feel
increasingly uncomfortable in her own skin as well as her living space. This was because the woman "was having a tough
time giving herself permission to go ahead, buy a place, decorate, live well. She who never took no for an answer at work
seemed paralyzed when it came to telling herself yes."

And why did she have this difficulty? Because she felt
uncomfortable in her own skin. In many different ways, we
hear composite echoes of one malady: women do not feel
comfortable in their own bodies, and then they extend this
sense of exile to the houses they inhabit. The sad, sorry,
silent, and heartbreaking truth is that many women don't
receive the gift of comfort—of *belonging*—when they cross
their threshold. And why? Because they think that they
don't deserve it. Where are you living now? Are you waiting for Prince Charming to come not just with a glass slip-
per but a matched set of Waterford crystal, china, and
complete window treatments?

Like many women I was raised to believe that the good
things in life—the roaring fire, the beautifully set table, the
delicious food, the good wine—are meant to be shared.
However, into the span of every woman's life comes a

solitary season or two—or even a decade—through choice, change, or circumstance. Why bother preparing the fire, cooking the meal, laying the table, opening a great vintage, if you're going to sip and sup alone? If no one is going to praise your pie, why bake it?

One of the most thrilling compliments I've ever received was from a Frenchman, who was not a lover but became a close friend. "You have a very sensual soul, Sarah." (Imagine it being said with a French accent. I'm still blushing.) When I asked why, he said, "You revel in your own pleasure. Your house wine is always a good vintage. You can tell more about a woman from the wine she serves when she's at home alone than you can from her perfume." We then had a wonderful conversation about the habit many people have of reserving "the best" for others, which has nothing to do with money— and everything to do with belief that personal pleasure is not important or that self-sacrifice is sacred.

Please don't waste the time I did, or feel embarrassed or hesitant about committing to establishing your House of Belonging and enjoying the best vintage you can afford, *now*. "Even if we're not flapping about with mates and chicks and all the little wormy things of life, we are still nesting," Dominique Browning reassures us. "We are giving ourselves shelter. Our work may be harder, but it is not less loving for being done alone." Going ahead on your own does not mean you're "shutting the door on the hope of finding true love," she says. In fact, it's the complete opposite. You're opening a new door to Love: the front door. There is a wonderful French fable, *La Petite Maison,* about a man who builds a house as a secret weapon for his seduction of beautiful women. He lavishes so much passion and attention on his house that women who cross his threshold swoon. You should know that feeling as well. And you will—by consciously choosing, if you must, to be gratefully home alone, dwelling in the House of Spirit.

FOR ALL WE KNOW

"The cream of enjoyment in this life is always impromptu. The chance walk; the unexpected visit; the unpremeditated journey; the unsought conversation or acquaintance."

—Fanny Fern

*I*t was about three months before I even left Newton's Chapel; my recuperation was very slow, but I was enjoying my home and began doing little things that I'd not allowed myself time to do for a decade. When life was not tidy, "it was the small things that helped, taken one by one and savoured," Rumer Godden had reminded me. I indulged in joyful simplicities that I adore: planting indoor bulbs, cleaning out closets and cupboards, creating a pretty little laundry room, experimenting with new recipes. I'd never spent as lengthy a time before in England, and, as I did, I began to notice more moments of contentment than distress. My Gratitude Journal from that time recalls, "the fire blazing while I was reading in bed on a cold, sleety night; the feeling of being safe and warm as the wind howled against the stone walls which had survived 900 years of huffing and puffing" and another strange entry, "I don't have to share my closets with anyone."

Still, I was at such a loss to understand why the second head injury had happened. I'm a woman who needs to make connections, and this one was taking quite a long time. Outside of Newton's Chapel, there's a very old apple tree, and I sit underneath it as often as I can, always leaning against the trunk. Each time I do, I'm struck by the happenstance that led me here, linking my ordinary daily round with one of the world's most cosmic coincidences: the apple falling from the tree while Sir Isaac Newton sat under it, disappointed and exhausted because every experiment he was doing so painstakingly right was going so terribly wrong. In the late summer and fall, when the fruit is heavy on the branch, I sit very carefully because apples tumble down regularly, and after sustaining two head injuries, I've got a thing about fast-moving objects. An apple falls down very directly, like that ceiling panel, like that suitcase. No veering to the left. No sashaying to the right. Plop. Plummet. Straight down. Newton had seen many apples drop before, but on that particular day during the summer of 1666, the apple's fall became a catalyst for one of science's most significant moments. Too tired to be anything but receptive, Newton understood this ordinary occurrence in a new light. Today Newton scholars discount the story as apocryphal, doubting its authority because it's too simplistic. But it's fascinating to me that the word *apocryphal*, which comes to us from the Greek, originally meant "hidden" and "secret." And indeed, Newton kept the story of the apple to himself for 20 years. Why had I tried so hard to keep the secret that I was just an ordinary woman, who found Grace in the miracle of gratitude and then lost her way because she wasn't grateful she was just human?

I was also so lonely now. "Shudder and sigh" lonely. I was a woman born for relationships, and yet to my great bewilderment, I was still alone. Then the moment came when there was no more room in my aching heart for keeping secrets from myself. To others, I effectively hid my secret sorrow, but the emotional exhaustion of carrying and concealing my loneliness became more than I could bear alone.

So I turned to Spirit. Knowing the transformative power of gratitude to redeem any situation, especially the impossible ones, I started a brand new Gratitude Journal. I began listing every reason I could think of to be grateful for the second head injury, for this Divine time-out, for the reversal of fortune, for being alone.

I have time for myself finally. I haven't lost all my money, I'm paying off my debts. Kate's tuition is paid. I have a beautiful home. I can eat anything in my own refrigerator at any time. I can spend Saturday reading and catch up on the housework whenever. I don't have to stop anything I'm doing to catch the score. Waxing can wait till spring (both floors and legs). I can spread all my papers and books on the other side of my bed and leave them there until I'm finished.

A few days later, it started to feel like an early spring. The poet David Whyte describes it so beautifully in his poem "The House of Belonging":

I awoke
this morning
in the gold light
turning this way
and that

thinking for
a moment
it was one
day
like any other.

But
the veil had gone
from my darkened heart
and I thought
it must have been the quiet
candlelight
that filled my room,

it must have been
the first
easy rhythm

with which I breathed
myself to sleep,

it must have been
the prayer I said
speaking to the otherness
of the night.

And I thought
This is the good day
You could
meet your love...

Well, I'd given up on days when I was going to meet my love. But I was at peace. But it *was* a good day to start spring cleaning. I was washing my kitchen window when I was struck by a thunderbolt thought: While it's wonderful to commit to another's happiness, it's *wondrous* to commit to your own. What would my life be like if I continued to be deeply devoted to my own well-being before another's? Really, that was what I'd been doing these last few months and it felt so *good*. This time-out had enabled me to glean some important information about myself—my passions, pleasures, peeves, points of view. If I wanted to be happy for the rest of my life, I needed a country life, not the Big City; I wanted horses, dogs. More walks. A kitchen garden. I could start small with pots. I really wanted to take that rare sheep course. The lambing season would begin soon.

So I stopped what I was doing, found the brochure, and made the call and got the last space in the class. In a month I would go on a weekend course. No more just talking about raising sheep!

What else? I wanted to paint again, design, and rethink my work, my gifts, my home. I started to feel so enthusiastic that it occurred to me, after I finished cleaning my windows, that after months of inactivity, I needed to ease myself into a little easy exercise. I could go for a long walk through the gardens of my favorite country house hotel a few miles away and then have afternoon tea. Well, why not?

Is there any feeling more thrilling than the return of joy? How does joy send up its slender shoots through the dense and rocky soil of disappointment and despair and around the weeds of regret? One minute, like a garden in the dead of winter, you are dormant, and life's compromises and complexities have become so tangled that your own growth is stunted. Then suddenly a warmth and light surround you, and even though nothing may have changed outwardly, once again you begin to feel a pulse.

I was enjoying my tea and delicious scones in the drawing room, entranced by my new page turner, *So You Want to Keep Sheep?* I gazed rapturously at the flock of heavily pregnant ewes in the nearby field, excited at the miraculous rebirth of hope bubbling up inside me, when a group of golfers passed by and walked into the bar. I barely looked up.

But then I got that funny sensation when you think you are being watched, so I looked around to find one of the men had come out of the bar and was staring at me in bemused fascination.

"I *know* you," he said, grinning.

He was very handsome, and he did look slightly familiar, but I couldn't place him. And at that moment, probably for the first time in my life, I didn't need to. I was absorbed in my own company, filled with my new dreams of self-sufficiency. All I had was all I needed at that moment and I was so grateful. Finally, I was living in the House of *my* Belonging. I had come home to my own soul shelter: Myself.

They say a woman's heart is in her home.

Now I knew better.

Now I knew that a woman's home *is* her heart.

So I smiled at the very handsome man, shook my head, and said, "Sorry, I don't think so." I tried to go back to my book, but he locked my gaze and wouldn't let go. His smile grew wider.

We both started to laugh.

DO TRY THIS AT HOME:
RE-IMAGINING YOUR DWELLING SPACE
WITH SIMPLE ABUNDANCE

*Before you pick up a hammer, a paintbrush, or the
real estate ads, take time to daydream. Walk through
the rooms where you eat, sleep, and live. Give thanks
as you sift and sort, simplify and bring order to the
home you have.*

—Simple Abundance

"The great thing to keep in mind when you think of
the place you live in is that it is your refuge. You
may not like it very much, you may hope to move soon. It
may be shabby, too large, too small," the English writer
Elizabeth Kendall wrote in *House into Home*, published in
1962. "But even if you're there only until next Friday, it is
still your refuge."

Well, unless you're literally in the middle of moving
house, the chances are very good that we'll both be living in
the same place come next Friday. But what should interest
us is *how* did you feel waking up in your house *this* morning? And how will you feel returning to your house *tonight*?
As you pull into the driveway or turn the key, will your Soul
begin to sigh with grateful pleasure? When you cross the
threshold, what dreams wait to welcome you? As you walk
through your home, are there some rooms that you just pass

through to get somewhere else? Are there rooms with closed doors? Why are they closed? Because you're the only woman on the planet with *more* space than you need? Or is it because you have so little space that it's impossible to store things properly in the rest of the house, so the spillage gets stashed, thrown, dumped, and left in the "little room" down the end of the hall?

"We move in and out of our homes as if they mean nothing to us, as if we mean nothing to them, as if that glorious feeling of *being alive* had nothing to do with living each day. Only now and then does something happen that causes us to comment with profound astonishment, 'That got me where I live,' " Kathryn L. Robyn scolds us mildly in her wonderful book *Spiritual Housecleaning: Healing the Space Within by Beautifying the Space Around You.* "Whatever the size and scope of it, you doubtless have a kitchen, a bathroom, a place to sleep, and a place to sit. You may do all this living in a one-room studio or in a towering estate with dozens of rooms. You may live in a tent. The size of your house is not related to the size of your soul, but the condition of your dwelling does present a picture of the condition of your being—body, mind, and spirit. Is it chaotic, spare, colorful, an afterthought? Are you a person who needs an unstructured environment, a clear routine, reminders of joy, space to feel? Does your house reflect or provide you with your needs? Could it do this better? Do you know what those needs are? Or are you ignoring that knowledge, restricting your ability to respond to the requirements of your being? Have you followed somebody else's rules and abandoned your own before you even knew what they were?"

In other words, are you home, honey? If not, then it's time to hone in on recalibrating our homing instincts using the *Simple Abundance* principles—Gratitude, Simplicity, Order, Harmony, Beauty, and Joy—as a creative and practical template. Perhaps it's time for you to take another look at where you live *as if you have never seen it before.* Let's walk through the rooms of our homes together today and look around using our gift of sight bifocally, as the French artist Paul Klee suggests: "One eye sees, the other feels." I'll use my kitchen to show you what I mean. Let's begin with *Gratitude.* When I walk into my kitchen, I can give you at least seven things that make me feel grateful the moment I walk in:

(1) The kitchen is large enough for a table to eat at and seats six. It's the first time in my life I have been able to do that, which proves that delayed gratification can be a very fine friend.

(2) I *love* my oak kitchen table and chairs.

(3) I love my Aga cooker, my old-fashioned cast iron stove that provides both warmth and cooking surfaces.

(4) The washed pale wooden cabinet doors still please me after five years; as does the green, teal, and red floral William Morris Arts & Crafts fabric I've used for curtains, shades, and the upholstered backs of my kitchen chairs.

(5) I have a dishwasher, an electric kettle, and a retro juicer (practically a religious experience to use every morning).

(6) The view from my kitchen windows allows me to

watch the antics of our two turtle doves, Tristan and Isolde, in their own House of Belonging.

(7) My fancy pantry!

Ah, I'm on a roll here.

But how do I *feel* when I'm in my kitchen—when I'm not just looking at it but actually cooking in it? Crowded, as if there's not enough space; uncomfortable because the lighting's not right; and I really don't do as much cooking as I would like, especially baking, because there's too little counter space. The kitchen was designed to look pretty (and it does), but it wasn't designed to cook in. By the way, I've just had this insight as we're in here. That's very interesting. I wonder why?

Well, here's what I think happens when we start to look at a room in our house through the prism of gratitude. *Gratitude calms you down.* Gratitude quiets down the incessant whining critic who hates everything about us, our lives and our homes, and doesn't even let us have a moment to focus on what's good about them. Gratitude creates a space where we can pause and just be. Be quiet. Be in the room. Be receptive. Be creative. Be whimsical. Be able to look with one eye seeing and the other one feeling. Like a gentle giant (think *Shrek*) making space for us as we pass through a crowd, Gratitude clears the way for us to say, "See, it's not that bad," so whatever it is we're looking at becomes exactly that: Not so bad. And then we're inspired in unexpected ways to make the "not so bad" even better.

Besides, our homes are living entities. How would *you* feel if someone you cared about was always finding fault at every chance? I've been there, I've lived in that place and don't ever want to go back; I'm starting to feel achy just remembering it. But *we* do exactly the same thing to our dwelling places, never even giving a thought about the bad vibrations we're creating, intensifying, and sustaining every day with our negativity. In fact, we're polluting ourselves!

Now think of how you'd feel if you were praised and complimented. Happy. Cooperative. Expansive. Why wouldn't the kitchen, or any room of your house you're working on, respond in a similar, positive fashion?

The English writer Jane Alexander tells a wonderful story in her book *Spirit of the Home: How to Make Your Home a Sanctuary.* She and her husband had just moved into a Victorian rectory that needed extensive renovation after years of neglect. From the first day, the house was "a catalogue of woes." But they had fallen in love with the possibility of the grand old house and the papers were signed, so they shrugged their shoulders and got on with it. However, "life was pretty grim those first weeks and months. Virtually every day something else went wrong and we were spending a small fortune on builders, plumbers, plasterers, and electricians. It felt as though the house was trying its level best to make us unwelcome, to force us to leave.... It was heart-rending. We were starting to loathe the house we had loved."

Then one day, something else happened, and Jane Alexander blew up in frustration and just starting screaming at the house. "What's the matter with you? What do want from us? We're trying our best; we're fixing you up. What's your problem!"

She was hardly expecting an answer, but the next thing she knew she got one. "In my head I heard the house reply: 'What's the point? You're just like all the rest. You like the look of me but you don't really care. When you find out how expensive I am to fix you'll just patch me up and then leave me. You don't bother to fix the damp; to mend the botched jobs. So why don't you just get out now and be done with it. I'm sick of it all.' "

Jane Alexander didn't know if it was her imagination, subconscious, or the house talking to her, but she was intrigued and held up her end of the conversation: "I tried to reassure it that we weren't fly-by-nights; that we might not stay forever but we would undertake to put right the house's wrongs. We have kept our promise to this proud old house and three years later it is a totally different place. It's not just that it's been freshly decorated and has a nice new kitchen, a good solid new roof, and strong replacement windows. It has a completely different atmosphere. You walk into the house and it feels comfortable, warm, and welcoming. I can never quite decide which favorite spot I will curl up in with a book. Friends love to come to stay and the house seems to laugh at the sound of children and dogs playing up and down its corridors…. It takes a shift of attitude but once you start the work it will probably feel curiously familiar. Take it slowly—you can't change everything at once—and remember that every house has its individual personality."

SIMPLIFY THIS HOUSE

*We want, we need, we desire, we yearn, but we
don't ask.... Longings cross our mind, but we don't
really commit ourselves. But when wishful thinking
doesn't magically manifest what we want, we feel
we've been denied.*

—*Simple Abundance*

Gratitude doesn't ask us to stay stuck in lack or live in denial but to acknowledge and accept the reality of our situation so we can get our bearings before moving on to our highest good.

The 19th-century New Zealand writer Catherine Mansfield reassures us, "Everything in life that we really accept undergoes a change." Then, Gratitude invites the next *Simple Abundance* principle, Simplicity, for her opinion.

So if today you feel uncomfortable in your kitchen, as I do, if the space is too small, cramped, narrow, dark, inconvenient, impractical, or ugly (you get the drift of the downward spiral), stop calling attention to the room's flaws and begin the process of re-imagining the room by finding five favorable qualities. Right now, before we go any further. Go ahead; list five good things about your kitchen:

(1)

(2)

(3)

(4)

(5)

Feel better? It's absolutely miraculous what a little shift of perception can do. Beginning to think of our homes as living, breathing, feeling entities requiring a loving, reciprocal relationship with their tenants is how to begin.

"When we look back at the places where we have lived during our life, we remember some with nostalgia and love while others we remember as places connected to unhappiness and pain. We often assume that the ups and downs of life are associated with the place where certain events in our life occurred," Suzy Chiazzari tells us in *The Healing Home*. "Most people leave it at that, never considering that the house and buildings themselves may have contributed to their feelings of discontentment or well-being. Buildings are essentially alive."

So I'm in the kitchen asking it what Simplicity might do for me here. The room tells me I have too many things cluttering up the space—the counters, the window ledges, open shelves. Indeed, most of my items are beautiful, but the room can't breathe, can't spread out, can't enjoy cooking. Oddly enough, that's how I feel when I'm trying to make dinner. But I love my collection of mixing bowls, teapots, and colorful china.

"Very pretty," the kitchen says. "Now you must clear the counters of *everything*."

"What?" I say. "I don't think I like where this conversation is going."

"Just try it for the weekend. See what you really miss, what you really need, how you feel tomorrow morning when you come down and the space is cleared. If the clear space doesn't *feel* better than the pretty clutter, then you can put it all back." The kitchen and Simplicity are in cahoots.

Well, it could be an interesting experiment. I'll give it a try. Why don't you do it too? It will be fun, instructive, and, no doubt, revealing.

Using Simplicity to re-imagine a room invites us to sift, sort, remove, as well as retain. It also encourages us to move the furniture! If you would rather see that chair *over there* or in another room even if it's been *here* for 15 years, move it! Is your space filled with excess baggage of old relation- ships—parents, siblings, roommates, lovers, or spouses, chil- dren who have moved out or a self that you parted from long ago? Are there pieces of furniture, equipment, knickknacks that might be stylish but don't resonate or reflect you any- more? In 20 years I've passed through my American Country phase and moved on to English Victorian, Arts and Crafts, Art Deco, Art Nouveau, English cottage, hodge- podge, streamlined, sophisticated, and rustic. Now I'm really trying to only keep items I feel passionate about because love is a great common denominator. Weed through your possessions and only keep or display what makes you smile and grateful to see or use. As a rule of thumb, the 19th- century English designer William Morris's maxim can't be beat: "Have nothing in your houses that you do not know to be useful or believe to be beautiful."

Order's in here now, rooting through the drawers, finding out how many duplicate egg slicers are jamming up the space. She's found three. But think Betty Boop instead of Nurse Crachitt, because this babe is smiling and humming as she bops to swing music playing on the radio. Before I know it, duplicates of everything are in the give-away box. I get to keep the one I like best, which is actually beautiful and useful. Many of the items I forgot I even had. It's like going shopping in your own closet and drawers; I'm exhilarated. Let's try another one.

On second thought, let's not. That's about all the focusing I can do today. I don't want to start something that I can't finish. Nor do you. Applying the *Simple Abundance* principles to the re-imagining of the rooms of our homes needs to be as gentle and gradual as the path itself. Please don't set yourself up for failure by attempting to do the whole house in a weekend. You won't be able to; you'll get tired and cranky and then frustrated and give up. Time will pass, and next year you'll still be living in chaos and clutter and reading another book on how to get your act together.

This is how we get our house together—one drawer, one cabinet, one shelf, one closet, one room at a time.

When it comes time to invite the fourth principle, Harmony, into your rooms, think of the word *comfort*. The secret to transforming dwelling places into havens is comfort. The idea you're going for is, when you're in your nest, you should feel so warm, cozy, and comfortable you don't want to leave any time soon. Where is your comfort default position? Do you only have one? Well, if you're living in a studio, one is an acceptable answer. If not, you should have a comfort nook in every room of your house. A place to read with your feet up, pay bills, daydream, take a nap, work on a craft project, and indulge in the serious soulcraft of taking care of yourself.

By the time you have worked with these four transformative principles in a room, you'll be stunned by how much *Beauty* has been right in front of your eyes that you couldn't see before. By the way, how well are you seeing in each room of your house? How much Light is there in your home? What an enormous mood shifter the right amount of light in a room provides! Always remember that invoking Light was the first command God gave when creating the Universe; I don't think we should do any less in our homes.

"We often hear that in near-death experiences people find themselves moving towards a brilliant light. But it's not just in death that we have this automatic response to light. In our everyday lives we humans have a strong built-in instinct to move towards light, which results in a significant sense of well-being," architect and writer Sarah Susanka reminds us in her wonderful primer, *Home by Design: Transforming Your House into Home.* "This is such a simple principle, yet it is also one of the most powerful. As you observe the world around you, you'll notice that in many of the places you find the most engaging, this principle is at play. Conversely, many of the places that feel the most oppressive are lacking it."

If there are glaring inadequacies about your lighting, you'll know it by how you physically feel. Do you have headaches trying to read? Is the intensity of light all one level (like in a discount supermarket), or can you balance the amount of light in a room? Are you taking full advantage of all the natural light available to you? Perhaps you'd *feel better* if you took down that beautiful curtain and tried letting as much sunlight as possible into your living room during the day and adding wooden shutters for privacy when the sun goes down.

Do you use candles for light at night? I've never known a room or a woman who didn't grow more beautiful by the glow of candlelight. Gather some together and light them tonight. Just be observant; notice how you feel by candle-light—how differently you choose what to do and how you do it. How does your conversation differ? Is it quieter, more intimate? Do you find yourself taking your activity level down a few notches? Good, we're making progress.

When I moved to the English countryside, my most surprising adjustment was learning to live according to the rhythm of natural light. Day is for activity, night is for rest. In the city, electricity makes it easy to blur the boundaries between day and night, and I do, usually by burning my candle at both ends. But on winter nights in the country, where I'm at the back of beyond, the only candles meant to be burning are on my kitchen table. Right now, as I write, daylight is fading. The shadows seem to whisper, *"Simmer down now."* By 5 o'clock the curtains are drawn, the fire is blazing, and the lamps are throwing off golden slivers that creep through the cracks between the windows and doors. The sixth *Simple Abundance* grace, Joy, has just arrived. She has a handsome woven basket filled with contentment, laughter, ease, and repose. Would I like to empty her basket and fill it with the cares of the day? Oh, yes, please. She'll put them down by the back door where they'll be waiting for me tomorrow. But for now, the conviviality of evening invites us not just to write or read about Joy but to live it. What a difference a decade can make!

NESTING INSTINCTS: ALL COMING BACK TO ME NOW

Love does not stop. Energy doesn't stand still. And neither do our homes. They're pulsing with all that we carry in; they vibrate, hum, resonate with every cry and murmur and snap and cheer of our hearts. They are our second skins, the shells we build, like snails, enlarging and encrusting with the whorls of our days, months, years. They are the most private and most telling of places. There they stand, for the world to see. And for us to make them what we will.

—Dominique Browning

An Englishman once commented at a dinner party that the most erotic fantasy he could imagine was the sight of Annette Bening vacuuming in her slip and rubber gloves in the film *American Beauty.* I thought it was a hilarious send-up. Well, it wouldn't be the first time one man's erotic fantasy made a woman laugh.

The most pleasurable way that I know to re-imagine the task of taking care of our homes, so they can take care of us, is by making a game out of it. By "playing house." Remember? Okay, which is it you've forgotten? Playing house or playing? "We usually think of play as self-indulgent and irresponsible," Diane Ackerman explains charmingly. In her mesmerizing book *Deep Play*, the scholar, scientist, siren, scribe, and Rennaissance woman breaks feminine silence and meditates on the sacred meaning of play in our lives.

Women will encourage their children to play because we know it's how a child learns to navigate her way through the universe. But when we grow up we dismiss one of life's most sacred experiences, just as we've discounted the role our homes truly play in our lives.

"A funny notion, feeling whole," Diane Ackerman muses. However, "in rare moments of deep play, we can lay aside our sense of self, shed time's continuum, ignore pain, and sit quietly in the absolute present, watching the world's ordinary miracles. No mind or heart hobbles. No analyzing or explaining. No questing for logic. No promises. No goals. No relationships. No worry."

One of my favorite ways of playing is puttering, that pleasant meandering of the mind when a woman is rearranging the objects that surround her. I don't know about you, but I can start dusting or straightening a crooked picture on the wall, and if I'm left to my own devices, I've lost a couple of hours and gained serenity. Instead of chores, how about playing house? Feel at a loss when it comes to transforming drudgery into reveries? Well, even clutter-busting can be fun with the right music (something with a beat) and the right costume. If your taste leans more towards blue gingham and sparkling red shoes, you go, girl, because Dorothy found her way home again in that garb. These days I'm playing French maid. Still, I don't take out the feather duster until I've hauled away at least one bag of unmentionables—this morning it was ratty linens and half-used bottles of beauty treatments from the bathroom. The bathroom is a great place to begin playing house. How many jars and tubes of beauty creams, lotions, and potions promising to lift, firm, smooth, shape, and rejuvenate your looks and your life are crowding your bathroom shelves? Unless you're planning to open up a day spa, you can *keep* three. While we're in there, let's clean out the makeup cabinet. If it's older than a year, or your age divided by 50, you know what to do. Eggplant eyelids and tangerine lips are so not *now,* nor will be for either of us *ever* again.

"Our homemaking skills haven't really been lost—they are simply crafts which have become rusty through disuse," Jane Alexander reassures us. "We can swiftly relearn the steps to creating a true home, to ensouling the home. All it takes is a little time and effort—and a large dose of imagination and wonder. What is needed is nothing less than the re-enchantment of our homes—to endow them with magic, warmth, and joy. We need to bring back the life and soul of the home, honour its power and healing, respect its spirit."

HEART REFLECTIONS:
THE BELOVED OFFERS A PSALM OF
PRAISE FOR HER HOUSE OF BELONGING

Mother of Eden, Architect of the Eternal, we rejoice in the magnitude of this moment. Your Beloved has met herself at the door of her heart's yearning and found Heaven hath gone before her to make welcome her approach. She has crossed the threshold of the House of her Belonging and warmed herself at the hearth of her own heart. Your Beloved is astonished by the Simple Abundance of her home comforts, giving the Dreamer of Domestic Bliss our prayer of thankfulness for leading her beyond the bewilderment of loss, past the straits of sorrow, across the desert of disappointment, into the sacred Shelter of Solace and the sanctuary of repose. Bless the foundation upon which her House of Belonging is built, fashioned from her own delights. Bless the cornerstone of gratitude, the sturdy walls of simplicity's stones, the bricks of balance, the mortar of loving memory. Paint the rafters with the hues of harmony, feather her nest with contented nuzzles, awaken her to the beauty of Light, Space, and Order. Nourish her at the celebrating table, and lift the cup of good cheer and much rejoicing. Let her laugh that all the world may be blessed by her merriment. May she rest, that she may once again be renewed, restored to Paradise Found. May her House of Belonging become a reflection of all that is lovely in this world and a refuge for all she loves on this earth.

Thank you for bringing your Beloved home.

Be it done by Grace, with all praise and honor according to Thee, and received with joy by She.

Home! May peace and plenty always be her portion. Home!

THE PLOTS OF GOD AND LOVE

The plots of God and Love are One and the same.

—Niall Williams

*H*appiness is much more difficult to write about than sorrow, just as the longing for love is easier to describe than its fulfillment. Still, I suspect that many writers secretly wish they could write from a deep well of happiness at least once just to know how it feels. I know I did. But the reality is when a writer's happy, the last thing she wants to do is dissect the ephemeral; she wants to exult in her euphoria, not explain the miracle. "There are times when Life surprises one," the Victorian writer Ellen Glasgow confessed, "and anything may happen, *even* what one had hoped for." Can you believe that?

My husband smiles as he asks, "You're happy, aren't you?" We just celebrated our first wedding anniversary. He knows the answer: Yes, I'm happier than I ever believed possible, but then I'm a True Believer in the Church of Improbable Happy Endings. And he—well, he's a lucky guy.

Thirty years ago I was working as a freelance fashion journalist in London. Making the rounds of parties was part of the job, especially during Fashion Week each spring and fall. One enchanted evening, my eyes met Jonnie's and we smiled. Like a movie scene, he walked towards me with a glass of Champagne. Jonnie was the quintessential English upper-class charmer with a voice to match. Devastatingly handsome, intelligent, sexy, and very funny in that seductive, self-deprecating way that disarms and delights American women of all ages. We struck up a conversation that had us laughing and wanting more, so we continued it the next day at lunch.

Jonnie had studied economics and law and worked as a risk management consultant in London's "The City" (like America's Wall Street). But he also raced cars, sailed, skied; played cricket and golf; rode horses; managed talent; speculated in real estate; and imported wine. He spoke French and Italian. He had piercing blue eyes, a cleft chin, and a wicked sense of humor. He made my knees knock. (Later I would learn that a red circle skirt, white fox boa, seamed stockings, high heels, and a saucy black cocktail hat with a veil had a similar effect on him.) He was also an unfailingly polite gentlemen who made sure he kissed all the girls so that none of them would feel left out. He was an outrageous flirt. But I'd have been disappointed if he hadn't been!

His memories: "A slim but curvy young American beauty, lively and vivacious—a journalist by profession and a charmer by disposition. Sarah was wonderfully literate, clear-thinking, and amusing. She was, as we English say, 'dead sexy,' and I recall noticing so from way across the crowded room. She had exquisite sparkling brown eyes, a ready smile, great legs, and more than good taste in high-fashion shoes. As we talked of our work, travels, pleasures, and friends, I quickly realized that we had many passions and interests in common. I also recall, regrettably, that at the time I was involved with another partner, and that in order to be honest and straight, we would have to walk away from each other or much hurt would be caused."

We were having a grand time at lunch when Jonnie suddenly became very quiet. "I like you, Sarah, I really do. I don't just fancy you, which I certainly do, but *I really like you.*"

Oh, dear.

"So I think I ought to tell you that I'm sort of involved…."

I said something that still astonishes me today: "I like you, too, Jonnie."

No time for coffee or second thoughts. Reluctantly we said, "It's been fun," and walked away from each other.

SURPRISED BY JOY

Fate brings its own clocks.

—Pearl Bailey

P sychics. What do they know? Well, this one knew it would be 30 years before true love came looking for me. From my journal:

Newton's Chapel. Valentine's Day 2003.

Another year in this lifetime begins and yet we are not together. Where are you? My heart's so restless. I must accept that, despite all my efforts to find you in this incarnation, I may not succeed. My deeper feelings, when I'm clear, know that this isn't true—and they help me to "see" that you are there for me if I'm willing to dismantle the barricades I've erected that keep me alone. Spirit's already done the heavy bulldozing. But as I rebuild my life, it's up to me not to dig a trench too wide or deep or to bar the door when Love knocks. I can't run away any more, my darling; my soul needs to be At Home. Heaven knows where we both are. I turn to the Holy Ones to help us find our way to each other. I ready my home, my things, my heart. I make space. I will even clean out a closet for you.

Newton's Chapel felt so welcoming when Jonnie drove me home that day. He lived a couple of hours away and had come to play golf on a spur of the moment. Like me, he had been divorced for several years and settled into never marrying again and was concentrating on the well-being of his children, his business, and his golf game.

Over the months we would marvel again and again at our

story: The twists and turns of three decades. The rediscovery
of love as ancient reunion and recognition—not as an act of
intent, will, fantasy, or fling. The mystery of my House of
Belonging being in England. How both of us had stopped
looking for love in all the wrong places and faces. How, if I
had not sustained the second head injury and spent time
recovering here, our paths would probably never have crossed.
How the plots of God and Love are one and the same thing.

Nothing is more mysterious, mystical, or magical than
falling in love, except preparing for its arrival. "The quest
for love is at the heart of much of our striving, yet it is not
striving that invokes it. Although there are no absolute
strategies for making love happen, and no surefire oracles
for predicting the time and place of its arrival, there are ways
in which one can prepare for it," Nancy Bauch and Michelle
Lizieri remind us in their tiny jewel of a book, *Awaiting a
Lover*. First, one must cultivate "the conditions of being that
will not only invite love but also encourage it to thrive."

It's been said that romance is unsatisfactory as a religion,
but as an approach to homemaking I know that romance
performs miracles. Think of the hustle and bustle around
the house when a potential sweetheart is coming to call for
the first time. Picking up, putting away, dusting, reposition-
ing objects *just so*, arranging flowers in a pretty vase—all
these small little touches become romantic foreplay.

Now imagine for a moment that you don't know Love is
about to call! If Love unexpectedly knocked on your door,
would you be too embarrassed by the household chaos to

answer? Could you ask Love to make himself comfortable, or would you have to dig out the chair from underneath the clothes, the videos, the stray shoe...? Could you open your refrigerator door and whip up something tempting, or does the thought make you cringe? When Love wants to wash off the dust from the long journey to your side, do you think the sink scum will enchant? What about the week's worth of newspapers strewn about the living room floor? Is it enough tinder to light Love's fire? Lucky then that I'd been spring cleaning before Love arrived unexpectedly.

THE GRACE OF RECOGNITION

> *Taking the bull by both horns he kissed her violently on her dainty face. My bride to be he murmured several times.*
>
> —Daisy Ashford (aged 9)
> *The Young Visitors* (1919)

Reader, I married him. In Newton's Chapel, standing beneath the 12th-century Norman arch, surrounded by our children and close friends. The bride wore a gown of lace and pink silk tulle. Katie gave her mother away. Jonnie's sons were his groomsmen. The cat refused to wear his black bow tie. The best man mislaid the wedding rings. Maybe that was because my husband gave me seven thin, interlocking gold bands—a wedding ring for every day of the week. There were tears of joy, much laughter, vintage Champagne under the bows of the apple tree, Red Velvet wedding cake, and fireworks. Our first dance was to Etta James singing "At Last." There were "carriages at midnight" for departing guests.

"Late in life, with indomitable courage, we continue to say that we are going to do what we have not yet done," the French philosopher and poet Gaston Bachelard confesses. "We are going to build a house." Building the House of Belonging is the soul's commitment to living a passionate life. Your Authentic Self is the architect. Your choices are the structural timbers; courage is the foundation stone; patience, perseverance, and self-permission are your bricks; faith is the mortar. The home where you live today may not be your dream house, but it does shelter your sacred dreams. Honor and protect them. Nurture your dreams of domesticity, and let them nourish you. As he explains, "If I were asked to name the chief benefit of the house I should say: The house shelters daydreaming, the house protects the dreamer, the house allows one to dream in peace."

At the beginning of this book, I shared my belief that we each have a House of Belonging waiting for us. I told you that every relationship you have—with other people, with your work, with Divinity—reflects in some way your Soul's intimate union with you! Then the House of Belonging expands to become your intimate surrounding—and the very feeling of safety, joy, and contentment that you experience in your home. An earthly home that charms, delights, enchants, embraces, sustains, and inspires you is part of Spirit's blueprint for your happiness.

Dusk has turned into twilight through a progression of

eventide hues right outside my window—steel gray to smoky blue to charcoal ash. Dark now, just in these last few minutes. And as dark as you have never seen dark before, unless you grew up in the country. Time to light the candles and throw another log on the fire. My lovely, warm, welcoming kitchen is too irresistible for any more words. She's waiting for me to open wide my heart to receive the gifts accumulating with my name on them.

And you, dearest reader? Are you open to receive your gifts? For when the six graces of *Simple Abundance* become your home's redecorators and renovators, you'll find yourself awakening in, and returning to, not just a dwelling place, but a soul shelter. A home of your own.

A House where you *Belong*.

The story of *your* heart is just beginning.

And may you live happily ever after.

The End

WITH THANKS AND APPRECIATION

...life itself is a story and we have to tell it in stories—that is the way it falls. I have told the truth and nothing but the truth, yet not the whole truth, because that would be impossible.

—Rumer Godden

Have you ever wondered how books come into being? "There are four ways to write a woman's life," the distinguished author and critic Carolyn G. Heilbrun explains in *Writing A Woman's Life.* The woman herself may tell it, in what she chooses to call an autobiography; she may tell it in what she chooses to call fiction; a biographer, woman or man, may write the woman's life in what is called a biography; or the woman may write her own life in advance of living it, unconsciously and without recognizing or naming the process.

With all of my books I have unconsciously opted for the last way, hurling myself out there on the page, not realizing what I've written until I find myself living it sometime in the future. So, too, was the creative process of *Moving On*. Not meant to be a book at all, quite frankly.

The house in Maryland was up for sale and I had to come over from England to clear it out. I was on my knees in the hot, dusty attic with hundreds of unmarked brown boxes that hadn't been opened in decades—boxes from my high school years, boxes from my years abroad in Europe during the 1970s, boxes sent on after both my parents died, boxes removed from the attic of the home I had shared with my daughter's father, boxes that had accumulated in the five years Kate and I lived on our own, and boxes of publishing memorabilia going back to my freelance years.

I'd been sifting, sorting, and throwing away for three weeks; I was a wreck and the movers were arriving in 48 hours. The attic looked as if I hadn't even started. That's because I could lose whole days caught in the vortex of remembering. Finally, my dearest chum, Dawne, whose friendship with me dates back to our single/white/female days as roommates, suggested I hire some college students to help pick up the momentum so that I couldn't stop and tell personal stories. She recommended her daughter, Abby, who possesses a razor-sharp wit that slices and dices sentimental blathering.

We came across a 10x10-foot space filled to the rafters with boxes of research files—material I'd used in some way or another on all my previous books stretching back to 1985. My shoulders slumped and my heart grew faint. "I guess we'll just have to ship that," I moaned.

"Do you even know what's in here?" Abby asked.

"No, but it's stuff I'd like to go back to before I write another book, just in case."

"Just in case what?"

"Just in case I don't know what I'm doing or saying. There's research in here I've probably never used."

"Oh, Auntie Babe, it's so time for new inspiration," the wag said as she started dropping the boxes down the stairs into the dumpster. "So time to move on…. Your readers will so thank me."

We laughed, and I chucked the next box. Oh, what the hell. I wasn't ever going to write another book again. What could I possibly have to say? So those two little words— "moving on"—became the mantra for the remainder of the upheaval, resettling, and removals in store for me. God bless your moxie and sass, Abby Winter. And may the Holy Mother bless your mother, who holds down the U.S. fort for Simple Abundance with such graciousness and good humor, making sure my mail gets answered. Dawne Winter, you are too, too marvelous for words. Whoever said no one is irreplaceable certainly never met this woman. I'm just sorry I had to spoil her plans to write her tell-all. Without the old material, I had to tell stories on myself. All you have left is the one with me dancing on the bar (I hope).

To the Great Creator, in whom I move, write, live, love, and find my being and my meaning, I offer my humble thanks for the gift of bringing this book into the world, especially after I was convinced that I could never, ever again experience passion on the page. My dear friend and literary agent, Chris Tomasino, guided my return to writing with unflinching belief in this book; her passion, intelligence, wit, warmth, and deep respect for my work over the last 18 years has moved me greatly. Our creative duo has been, and continues to remain, among my life's most wonderful blessings, and your name will always grace my Gratitude Journal.

To my wonderful sister, Maureen O'Crean, thank you for your assistance with our website and your devotion to all the *Simple Abundance* fans. I am indebted to Susan Leon, for sharing the pivotal points in other women's lives as they chose to move on.

My great thanks to Linda Cunningham, Editorial Director, Trade Books, at Meredith Books, for inviting me to move on to the next chapter of my publishing career with Meredith. Linda was an editor on my first book, *Mrs. Sharp's Traditions,* and it's such a pleasure to work with her again.

Among my great blessings at Meredith has been the guidance and contribution of my editor, Denise L. Caringer, whose concern for the writer, as well as the book, always gave me just the encouragement I needed at the perfect moment, and who has preserved so beautifully the illusion that I am in command of the English language. Bless you, Denny.

To everyone else on the Meredith team, including Erin Burns, Matt Strelecki, and Greg Kayko who moved Heaven and earth to make sure we ended up with a beautiful book, and to the sales team who has shown such enthusiasm in letting the booksellers know I'm back, many thanks.

To Oprah Winfrey, Simple Abundance's Godmother and my work's most generous supporter over the last decade, thank you. Meister Eckhart was right, but "thank you" hardly seems enough. Bless you for shielding my privacy while I needed space and time to heal these past few years so that I could move on. You will always have my deepest gratitude, appreciation, and love.

There are no words to convey my gratitude and love to my cherished daughter, Katherine Sharp. You have so graciously grown up with nine books as your siblings and have always been such a part of every word I've ever written. Bless you, sweetheart. My heart returns the raw material of your own life back to you now; thank you for letting me share our lives with the rest of the world. As you embark on your own brilliant career as a filmmaker, may you always hear and trust the Deeper Vibration, so that your stories become for others the gift of Grace that your life has been for me.

To my stepsons, Alexander Carr and Charles Carr, thank you for generously and good-humoredly keeping your father company on so many Sundays when I had to work on this book. You guys made it possible for me to write a few more pages without guilt.

But the heart and soul of this book's inspiration is expressed in my dedication to my husband, Jonathan Donahue Carr, without whose unconditional love, unwavering belief, and unflagging support *Moving On* could not have been started or finished. There were so many moments in which this book became the bridge too far. Each time I faltered, he carried me across safely. God bless and keep you, my darling, on this, our first wedding anniversary. Here, with my dearest love and gratitude, is a gift of paper. I only pray that, now and always, you'll be able to read between every line more than mere words can ever say.

Sarah Ban Breathnach
Newton's Chapel
30 October 2005

ABOUT THE AUTHOR

S arah Ban Breathnach (pronounced "Bon Brannock") celebrates quiet joys, simple pleasures, and everyday epiphanies. She is the author of 10 books, including the two #1 *New York Times* best-selling titles, *Simple Abundance* and *Something More*. *Simple Abundance* was named one of the top 10 best-selling books in the United States during the 1990s, according to *USA Today*.

Sarah Ban Breathnach is also the President and CEO of Simple Abundance®, Inc., a consultancy firm specializing in publishing and multimedia projects that give creative expression to the Simple Abundance® principles and to the concept of personal authenticity. She has been named one of America's "most fascinating women of power and influence" (*George* magazine, 1998). Sarah Ban Breathnach is the founder of the Simple Abundance Charitable Fund (SACF), a nonprofit bridge group between charitable causes and the public; the Fund is dedicated to increasing awareness that "doing good" and "living the good life" are soul mates. Since 1995 the SACF has supported the vision of more than 100 nonprofit organizations by awarding over $1 million in financial support. The Simple Abundance Charitable Fund is underwritten with proceeds from Sarah's speaking engagements, royalties, and product sales.

Sarah lives in the English countryside with her husband, Jonathan Donahue Carr.

Sarah Ban Breathnach would love to hear from you! Her new address is:

Simple Abundance
P.O. Box 77420
Washington, D.C. 20013

Or visit her on the web at *www.simpleabundance.com.*

Sarah Ban Breathnach offers a limited number of lectures, workshops, and private retreats in the United States and in residential retreats in Great Britain. Please contact her for more information.

SELECTED BIBLIOGRAPHY

*I only read what I am hungry for at the moment
when I have an appetite for it, and then I do not
read, I eat.*

—Simone Weil,
Waiting for God (1950)

M y soulful sustenance and sources for quotes have been many and varied. Collecting the pithy and the profound has been a passion of mine for more than 30 years, and I gather and glean from many sources: books, magazine articles, reviews, newspaper features, television broadcasts, plays, and film. However, my favorite collections of quotations for this book have been *The New Beacon Book of Quotations by Women* compiled by Rosalie Maggio (Boston: Beacon Press, 1996); *Bartlett's Familiar Quotations,* 16th ed., edited by Justin Kaplin (Boston: Little, Brown, 1992); *The Oxford Dictionary of Quotations,* 5th ed., edited by Elizabeth Knowles (Oxford, Oxford University Press, 1999); and Charlotte Moss's collection, *The Poetry of Home* (New York: Boxwood Press, 1998).

Abraham, Laurie, Mary Beth Danielson, Nancy Eberle, Laura Green, Janice Rosenberg, Carroll Stoner. *Reinventing Home: Six Working Women Look at Their Home Lives.* New York: Plume/Penguin, 1991.

Ackerman, Diane. *Deep Play,* New York: Random House, 1991.

A Natural History of the Senses. New York: Vintage Books, 1991.

Alexander, Jane. *Spirit of the Home: How to Make Your Home a Sanctuary.* London: Thorsons, 1998.

Allende, Isabel. *Aphrodite: A Memoir of the Senses.* New York: HarperFlamingo, 1998.

Ashford, Daisy. *The Young Visitors or Mr. Salteena's Plan.* London: Chatto & Windus. 1951.

Avakian, Arlene Voski, ed. *Through the Kitchen Window: Women Writers Explore the Intimate Meanings of Food and Cooking.* Boston: Beacon Press, 1997.

Bachelard, Gaston. *The Poetics of Space.* Boston: Beacon Press, 1994.

Ban Breathnach, Sarah. *Romancing the Ordinary: A Year of Simple Splendor.* New York. The Simple Abundance Press/Scribner, 2002.

Sarah Ban Breathnach's Mrs. Sharp's Traditions: Reviving Victorian Family Celebrations of Comfort and Joy. New York: The Simple Abundance Press/Scriber, 2001.

Simple Abundance: A Daybook of Comfort and Joy. New York: Warner Books, 1995.

The Simple Abundance Journal of Gratitude. New York: Warner Books, 1997.

Something More: Excavating Your Authentic Self. New York: Warner Books, 1998.

Bauch, Nancy and Michelle Lizieri. *Awaiting a Lover.* New York: Viking, 2000.

Bernstein, Frances, *Classical Living: Reconnecting with the Rituals of Ancient Rome.* San Francisco: HarperCollins, 2000.

Berriault, Gina. *Women in Their Beds: New and Selected Stories.* Washington, D.C.: Counterpoint, 1996.

Bridges, William. *Transitions: Making Sense of Life's Changes.* Cambridge, Mass.: Da Capo Press/Perseus Books, 2004.

The Way of Transition: Embracing Life's Most Difficult Moments. Cambridge, Mass.: Da Capo Press/Perseus Books, 2001.

Browning, Dominique. *Around the House and in the Garden: A Memoir of Heartbreak, Healing, and Home Improvement,* New York: Scribner, 2002.

Cameron, Julia. *The Artist's Way: A Spiritual Path to Higher Creativity*. New York: Tarcher/Putnam, 1992.

The Vein of Gold: A Journey to Your Creative Heart. New York: Tarcher/Putnam, 1996.

Campbell, Alexandra. *Remember This*. London: Penguin Books Ltd., 2005.

Campbell, Nina and Caroline Seebohm. *Elsie de Wolfe: A Decorative Life*. New York: Clarkson Potter, 1992.

Cantwell, Mary. *Manhattan Memoir*. New York: Penguin Books, 1996.

Chiazzari, Suzy. *The Healing Home: Creating the Perfect Place to Live with Color, Aroma, Light and Other Natural Elements*. London: Ebury Press, 1998.

Colwin, Laurie. *Home Cooking: A Writer in the Kitchen*. New York: Harper Perennial, 1993.

More Home Cooking: A Writer Returns to the Kitchen. New York: HarperCollins, 1993.

Crawford, Ilse. *Home Is Where The Heart Is*. London: Quadrille, 2005.

The Sensual Home: Liberate Your Senses and Change Your Life. London: Quadrille, 1997.

Cunningham, Laura Shaine. *Sleeping Arrangements*. New York: Riverhead Books, 2000.

De Bastide, Jean-Francois. *The Little House: An Architectural Seduction*. Translation by Rodolphe el-Khoury. New York: Princeton Architectural Press, 1996.

de Wolfe, Elsie. *The House in Good Taste*. New York: Rizzoli, 2004.

Didion, Joan. *Slouching Towards Bethlehem*. New York: Farrar, Straus and Giroux, 1968.

The Year of Magical Thinking. London: Fourth Estate, 2005.

Dunn, Mary. "The Queen Was in the Kitchen." In *The Years of Grace: A Book for Girls,* edited by Noel Streatfield. London: Evans Brothers Limited, 1950.

Dwight, Eleanor. *Edith Wharton: An Extraordinary Life*. New York: Abrams, 1994.

Fisher, M.F.K., *With Bold Knife and Fork*. New York: Smithmark, 1996.

Ford, Debbie. *Spiritual Divorce: Divorce as a Catalyst for an Extraordinary Life*. New York: HarperCollins, 2001.

Friedan, Betty. *The Feminine Mystique*. New York: Dell, 1964.

Fussell, Betty. *My Kitchen Wars: A Memoir*. New York: North Point Press, 1999.

Garner, Lesley. *Everything I've Ever Done That Worked*. London: Hay House, 2004.

Godden, Rumer. *A House with Four Rooms*. London: Macmillan, 1989.

Gould, Joan. In *Hers: Through Women's Eyes: Essays from the 'Hers' Column of the New York Times,* edited by Nancy R. Newhouse. New York: Villard, 1985.

Graham, Ysenda Maxtone. *The Real Mrs. Miniver: Jan Struther's Story*. London: John Murray, 2001.

Hampton, Mark. *Mark Hampton on Decorating*. New York: Random House, 1989.

Heilbrun, Carolyn G. "Unmet Friends." In *The Last Gift of Time: Life Beyond Sixty*. New York: Dial Press, 1997.

Writing a Woman's Life. New York: W.W. Norton and Co., 1988.

Herrmann, Dorothy. *Anne Morrow Lindbergh: A Gift for Life*. New York: Penguin Books, 1993.

Hillyer, Elinor. *Mademoiselle's Home Planning Scrapbook*. New York: Macmillan Company, 1946.

Horsfield, Margaret. *Biting the Dust: The Joys of Housework*. New York: St. Martin's, 1998.

Kaplan, Fred. *The Singular Mark Twain: A Biography*. New York: Doubleday, 2003.

Kendall, Elizabeth. *House into Home*. London: J.M. Dent, 1962.

Ladd, Mary-Sargent. *The Frenchwoman's Bedroom*. New York: Doubleday, 1991.

Lawlor, Anthony. *A Home for the Soul: A Guide for Dwelling with Spirit and Imagination*. New York: Clarkson Potter, 1997.

Lindbergh, Anne Morrow. *Dearly Beloved*. London: Chatto & Windus, 1963.

   Gift from the Sea. New York: Vintage Books, 1991.

Matthews, Caitlin. *Celtic Devotional: Daily Prayers and Blessings*. New York: Harmony Books, 1996.

McGinley, Phyllis. *Sixpence in Her Shoe*. New York: Macmillan, 1964.

Mendelson, Cheryl. *Home Comforts: The Art and Science of Keeping Home*. New York: Scribner, 1999.

Moore, Thomas. *The Re-Enchantment of Everyday Life*. New York: HarperCollins, 1996.

Murray, Elizabeth. *Cultivating Sacred Space: Gardening for the Soul*. San Francisco: Pomegranate, 1997.

Myss, Carolyn. *Spiritual Madness: The Necessity of Meeting God in Darkness*. Boulder, Colo.: Sounds True. 1997. Audiocassettes.

Norrington-Davies, Tom. *Cupboard Love: How to Get the Most Out of Your Kitchen*. London: Hodder & Stoughton, 2005.

Norris, Gunilla. *Being Home: Discovering the Spiritual in the Everyday*. New York: Bell Tower, 1991.

O'Donohue, John. *Anam Cara: A Book of Celtic Wisdom*. New York: Cliff Street, 1997.

Pagram, Beverly. *Folk Wisdom for a Natural Home*. North Pomfret, Vt.: Trafalgar Square, 1997.

   Home & Heart: Simple, Beautiful Ways to Create Spirit, Harmony, and Warmth in Every Room. Emmaus, Penn.: Rodale Press, 1998.

Paris, Ginette. *Pagan Meditations: Aphrodite, Hestia, Artemis*. Woodstock, Conn.: Spring Publications, Inc., 1986.

Rainbow, Elizabeth. "Posy and the Hopefuls" in *Calling All Girls!* 1955.

Robinson, Marilynne. *Housekeeping*. New York: Noonday Books, 1997.

Robyn, Kathryn L. *Spiritual Housecleaning: Healing the Space Within by Beautifying the Space Around You*. Oakland, Calif.: New Harbinger Publications, 2001.

Scott-Maxwell, Florida *The Measure of My Days*. New York: Knopf, 1968.

Seton, Nora. *The Kitchen Congregation: A Memoir*. London: Weidenfeld & Nicolson, 2000.

Sexson, Lynda. *Ordinarily Sacred*. Charlottesville: University of Virginia, 1992.

Shain, Merle. *Some Men Are More Perfect Than Others*. New York: Bantam, 1973.

Shenk, David. *The Forgetting: Alzheimer's: Portrait of an Epidemic*. New York: Doubleday, 2001.

Sinetar, Marsha. *Reel Power: Spiritual Growth Through Film*. Ligouri, MO: Triumph Books, 1993.

Steinem, Gloria. *Revolution from Within: A Book of Self-Esteem*. Boston: Little, Brown, 1992.

Stoddard, Alexandra. *Creating a Beautiful Home*. New York: William Morrow, 1992.

Struther, Jan. *Mrs. Miniver*. London: Virago Press, 1989.

Try Anything Twice. London: Virago Press, 1990.

Sullivan, Rosemary. *Labyrinth of Desire: Women, Passion and Romantic Obsession*. Washington, D.C.: Counterpoint, 2001.

Susanka, Sarah. *Home by Design: Transforming Your House into Home*. Newton, CT: The Taunton Press, 2004.

Tapert, Annette. *The Power of Glamour*. New York: Crown, 1998.

Thurman, Judith. "A Boudoir of One's Own." In *Victoria Magazine* (August 1992).

White, Michael. *Isaac Newton: The Last Sorcerer*. Reading, Mass.: Addison-Wesley, 1997.

Whyte, David. *Crossing The Unknown Sea: Work as a Pilgrimage of Identity*. New York: Riverhead Books, 2002.

The House of Belonging. Langley, Wash.: Many Rivers Press, 1996.

Williamson, Marianne. *Enchanted Love: The Mystical Power of Intimate Relationships*. New York: Simon & Schuster, 1999.

Wilson, Margery. *The Woman You Want to Be*. Philadelphia: Lippincott, 1942.

Windsor, The Duchess of. *The Heart Has Its Reasons: Memoirs of the Duchess of Windsor*. London: Michael Joseph, 1956.

Winspear, Jacqueline. *Birds of a Feather: A Maisie Dobbs Mystery*. London: John Murray, 2005.

WITH APPRECIATION AND PERMISSION

Enough, Friend.
If you want to read on,
Then go, yourself, become the book
and its essence.

—Angelus Silesius